Departures

A comedy in ten airports

John Godber

Samuel French — London
New York - Toronto - Hollywood

ISBN 0 573 01990 8

Please see page iv for further copyright information

DEPARTURES

First performed by the Hull Truck Theatre Company at the Sheffield Lyceum Theatre, on 4th September 2001, with the following cast of characters:

Jim	Iain Rogerson
Claire	Sherry Baines
Annie	Liz Carney
Steve	Rob Angell
Zoë	Liz Carney
Eva	Sherry Baines
Anita	Sherry Baines
Alison	Liz Carney
Dan	Rob Angell

Directed by John Godber
Designed by Pip Leckenby

CHARACTERS

Jim, managing director, 44
Claire, Jim's wife, 39
Annie, Jim's student daughter, 24
Steve, finance director, 45
Zoë, P.A. to Jim and Steve, 23
Eva, Czech hooker, 43
Anita, an official of Belgium Air, 40
Alison, works for American Airways, 25
Dan, American Airlines pilot, 45

Other plays by John Godber
published by Samuel French Ltd

April in Paris
Blood Sweat and Tears
Gym and Tonic
Happy Families
It Started With a Kiss
Lucky Sods
Men of the World
Passion Killers
Perfect Pitch
Salt of the Earth
Teechers
Thick As A Brick
(with music by John Pattison)
Unleashed
Up 'n' Under
Up 'n' Under II
Weekend Breaks

ACT I

Scene 1

Alicante Airport. Evening

The Lights come up on an airport departure lounge. However, the set is not so specific, it could be a departure lounge and it could be any other area of an airport. We should also get the feeling that the departure lounge is not at one particular airport. They all have a faceless sense of modernism. It could be any airport anywhere in the world; for the sake of this first scene it is the departure lounge of Alicante airport, Spain

Jim, a well-liked and affable forty-four-year-old is sitting next to Steve, a slightly older and a little more cynical colleague. The pair of them work for their own corporate video-making company, but the company is in its infancy and they are not big players. Jim sits and reads a book, Steve sits and reads the paper. Nearby, Eva, a lady with dark glasses, sits and reads a large airport novel with her back to the audience

We hear the bing-bong of the tannoy. Spanish departure times are called out. These are indecipherable to Jim and Steve. Jim stands and listens hard. Nothing

Jim What?
Steve Hang on!
Jim Sssh!
Steve What did she say?
Jim Hang on…
Steve Sssh!
Jim What?
Steve Sshh!
Jim Bollocks!

Music

Fade Lights

Scene 2

Alicante Airport. Slightly later the same evening

The Lights come up on Jim who is now standing over by the side of the stage. Steve still reads the paper and relaxes. The lady with the glasses reads. We hear the tannoy system deliver Spanish announcements once more. Jim and Steve try to make it out

Jim Ssssh!
Steve Hang on!
Jim Sssh!
Steve What's she on about?
Jim (*trying to listen*) No...
Steve Sssh!
Jim Not a clue!
Steve This is crackers.
Jim I'm going to get it next time.

Music

Fade Lights

Scene 3

Alicante Airport. Some time later the same evening

The Lights come back up on Jim and Steve

Jim stands looking into the fourth wall. Steve is standing upstage. Jim is anxious, and slightly drunk. Steve is quite calm

Jim Six bloody hours!
Steve Have another drink!
Jim I've got to drive when we get back!
Steve If we get back!
Jim Trapped in Alicante!
Steve Time is it?
Jim What a bloody nightmare! Claire'll go mad. She said this trip was a waste of time!

A beat

Steve All the other flights have gone, I think!
Jim Bloody excellent this is. Stuck here with two hundred pissed-up nutters!

Zoë enters. She is a young effusive holiday rep

Zoë Been looking for you two!
Jim Well, we're still here!
Zoë All the others are up at the bar.
Jim That's why we're down here!
Zoë It could be bad news, I'm afraid!
Jim What?
Zoë Well, they're saying that it could be cancelled actually.

A beat

Jim Oh, fuuuuckinn!
Zoë That's why I've come through. They've let me come through to tell you.
Jim So what's that mean?
Zoë Nobody knows yet…
Jim Bloody great…
Zoë I am sorry about this…
Jim What is it, a technical fault or the weather or what?
Zoë We're trying to find out.
Steve If it's a technical fault, don't tell him!
Jim This is just … a fuucckkinnn…
Zoë Sorry.
Jim So are we going to be stuck here overnight?
Zoë I don't know yet…
Jim Oh, wonderful!
Zoë I suppose it could be worse!
Jim No, it couldn't, I'll tell you that much. I hate flying as it is, and to make us wait six hours without a word or kiss my arse, is frankly outrageous…
Zoë I think there have been some announcements!
Jim Nobody can hear a friggin' word!
Zoë Well, they are trying.
Jim Nobody out here has got a clue what she's on about.
Zoë Well, some of it is in Spanish!
Jim Even the bloody Spanish can't understand it!
Zoë Well, like I say, I'm sorry but it's not really my fault!
Jim Well, it's somebody's fault and in the absence of some greater being I'm blaming you, all right?
Steve Hey hey…
Zoë I'm really sorry, I've come through to let you know, I shouldn't even be here!

Jim I know, I know, I'm sorry ... but——

A beat

Zoë I mean, obviously I'll go back and have another chat, but you know what it's like...
Jim What a bloody mess...

A beat

Zoë Did you get what you came for then?
Steve More than we bargained for!
Zoë What is it, a film?
Steve No, it's a training video for a Spanish hotel group.
Jim I only hope this airline never asks us for a video on customer services, we've got enough material to make a stinker.
Zoë So is it your firm, then?
Steve Just us two, we do everything on the cheap.
Jim That's the only reason we came out with this lot, because of the price.
Steve That's the bit we liked the best, isn't it? The price!
Jim I thought you liked Janice from Burnley the best?
Steve Well, yes, she was all right! And Sally from Cardiff, she was good fun.
Jim Until she broke her leg!
Steve What was she doing anyway?
Zoë Walking on a balcony drunk!
Steve Well, it's what you do, isn't it?
Zoë She was called Sally from Cardiff at the beginning of the week and by the end of the week everybody was calling her Seven Up, did you spot that?
Jim Oh ay, we spotted that.
Steve And that was with a pot on her leg.
Jim It's a good job she had a pot on or she might have broken a world record!
Zoë Janice is up by the bar if you're looking for her?
Steve No, I'll stay down here...

A beat

Zoë Well, I just wanted to let you know what was going on...
Steve Are you here all season, then?
Zoë I'm looking to get out ... it's not really...
Steve Looking for something else?
Zoë Well, my degree's in media studies! Listen, I'll go and see what's happening. I'm running round like somebody not right at the minute, I mean there's a bus full out there waiting to go to Benidorm, and we've lost the bloody driver!

Zoë exits

Jim and Steve have found her vivacious and attractive

Steve Got to have some metal to deal with all that lot.
Jim How did we end up with them?
Steve It's been a laugh, man!
Jim A laugh? When they took us into the mountains and got the pellet guns out I was ready for home. I mean getting pissed up and firing pellet guns at each other? Which genius thought that up? And what about that buggy ride up the mountains with Donna and Donna the Kebab sisters? I thought they were going to rape us! We're supposed to be working, you know?
Steve It's good to relax.
Jim Well, I haven't relaxed. I've been on edge all week.
Steve I could see that! I think everybody got off with everybody else. I even thought you and the Head Rep looked very friendly.
Jim Only talking!
Steve There's always a first time.
Jim No, Claire would be able to tell, as soon as I walked through the door.

Zoë returns. She looks like the bearer of bad news

Steve and Jim sense this

Zoë Bad news, I'm afraid. It looks like they're going to have to wait for another one to come in from Munich.
Jim So when's that?
Zoë It looks like five-thirty.
Jim Oh...
Zoë Tomorrow morning.
Jim Oh fuccckinnn...
Steve So we're not flying tonight?
Zoë I'm afraid not.
Jim That's it. I don't know whether to laugh or cry!
Zoë There's a complimentary drink at the bar.
Jim (*sarcastically*) Oh, well, that's all right then.
Zoë I can get you a voucher if you're interested.
Steve You'd better get us ten each!
Zoë Sorry! I did all I could! I'll have to go, I've got to get this coach off. Sorry.

Zoë exits

Jim and Steve remain still

Steve To the bar, then, to see Janice and Sally?

The bing-bong Spanish voice is heard once more. Jim is astonished

Jim Here we go!
Steve What is she on about?
Jim She says the flight's delayed and we'll have to sleep with the Kebab sisters, Janice from Burnley, and the lovely Sally the Seven Up!
Steve Well, I don't like mine so much.
Jim Well, I'll have to have yours, then!

Jim and Steve laugh at each other's jokes. They collect their belongings and slowly exit off upstage

Steve Oh, come on, laugh at it!
Jim I am laughing, look… (*He laughs like a maniac*) I'm laughing my head off!

Music

Fade Lights

Scene 4

Munich. Four weeks later, day

Claire, Jim's Claire, enters. She is wheeling a trolley with a number of cases and ski equipment piled high. She looks around the space. She sits down and looks at her watch. She looks at her boarding cards

Jim enters. He is dressed in track suit bottoms with a skiing type of top

Claire is quite relaxed and confident, she reads a magazine easily whilst Jim agitates

Claire Where've you been?
Jim Drifting about!
Claire Have you had one of them tablets?
Jim About an hour ago.

A beat

Claire I mean, I'm not wild about it myself, so…

Jim and Claire sit and relax

I'm exhausted, are you?
Jim Fresh air, isn't it?

A beat

Claire Different to Spain?
Jim Colder!
Claire Why you had to go out for a full week is beyond me!
Jim It was just as cheap, wasn't it?
Claire So what's happening with this Zoë, then?
Jim Steve's still trying to get hold of her.
Claire Oh ay!
Jim Nice lass, actually. And I think he's right, we need some support with all these European contacts taking off.
Claire Somebody for Steve to get his hands on, you mean?
Jim Well, she's pretty, but...
Claire Well, she would be, if he's involved...
Jim Yes, he's still a bit unreconstructed, is old Steve!
Claire And that's putting it mildly!
Jim I think she'll be good... She's a people person.
Claire As opposed to what?
Jim I dunno, but that's what they say, isn't it?

A beat

Claire I've really enjoyed it, have you?
Jim Well, yes, but the flight out was a bit...
Claire That was a good flight.
Jim Who did we fly with?
Claire Jat Air!
Jim Jat Air, you know what that means in English, don't you? Air Shit!
Claire It was OK.
Jim It was a military plane, wasn't it?
Claire It's mostly unspoilt out here, you know?
Jim (*walking downstage*) The plane wasn't! (*He looks out front*) That side is all clear and that side is all cloudy, which way do you think we'll be flying?
Claire It's only three hours anyway.
Jim Nearly four!
Claire Three and three quarters.
Jim Nearly four! (*He surveys the weather*) Goor, it looks black out there!
Claire Go and have a look to see if there's anything for my mum, will you?

Jim There's hardly any duty-free here, is there? There's no tannoy system either, they come and tell you when to get on! You have to pack the plane yourself apparently. The in-flight service was a bit of a let down and all!

Claire What did you expect?

Jim I mean I'm not a snob, but a bag of peanuts thrown at you by a woman with a beard isn't exactly Club Class, is it?

Claire It wasn't that bad.

Jim She had a beard! And then to be struck by lightning on the way out here, that was the best bit.

Claire It must happen…

Jim It did happen! It happened to us! And what did the pilot do? Nothing! Not a word from him until we'd landed and then he announces over the tannoy, very sheepishly "We have landed." Like it was a surprise to him.

Claire That's when everyone clapped!

Jim It was a bloody surprise to me to be honest. He was swinging it about like a kite. The fat bloke at the side of me was sweating like a pig, and I had no leg room… I could hardly get my seat tray down to eat my peanuts.

A beat

Claire Why don't you go and have a coffee?

Jim If we could just get on, I'd be fine, it's all the farting about waiting.

Claire You've never liked it, have you?

Jim I'm getting worse!

Claire I just put my mind off it.

A beat

Jim I bet it's just as quick to drive.

Claire How is it?

Jim Well, you have to get up early, then get to the check-in. Let's say that's four hours, let's say there's a delay five hours. Then a four hour flight.

Claire Three and three quarters!

Jim That's thirteen hours, and then another five hours waiting for your luggage.

Claire It never takes that long.

Jim And then getting your car, another hour and then from Manchester three hours if the traffic's good! What's that, a day? That's another thing they don't put in the brochure. (*He is still more interested in the sky*)

Claire reads

He must have to come right over the mountains at this side and then right up and turn left.

A beat

Claire I spoke to Annie by the way.
Jim She OK?
Claire She was in Prague, on her way to Amsterdam.
Jim I don't know how she does it!
Claire It's like getting on a bus for her.
Jim A first class honours degree. Bloody hell, I can remember when she was sick on the way to Mablethorpe!
Claire Twenty-two.
Jim Twenty-two.
Claire Where does it go?
Jim It just goes!
Claire Twenty years of flying and you're still a wreck.
Jim We haven't been flying for twenty years. When we first met, it was English holidays only.
Claire Because you wouldn't go abroad!
Jim I wanted to see England first.

Jim sits with Claire, they are quite close. And for a moment Jim's anxiety disappears

Claire Can you remember that chalet in the Lakes?
Jim What chalet?
Claire That chalet in the Lake District…
Jim It was a shack!
Claire It said chalet.
Jim It says zoom off to the Alps but we've just disproved that!
Claire You're never romantic, are you.
Jim I am, darling, but I got fleas, can you remember?
Claire You did, didn't you?

A beat

Jim I'll go and see if the wind's getting up!
Claire Why can't you sit down?
Jim I can't … my teeth rattle.
Claire Ha ha.
Jim No, they do, I think I've got a loose tooth.
Claire Honestly…?

A beat

Jim Do you think I should have another one of these tablets?

Claire How many have you had?
Jim Two.
Claire How many did the doctor tell you to take?
Jim One.
Claire Well, why have you had two?
Jim He just said it takes the edge off, it's like having a brandy, he said. They're non-addictive.
Claire Your Mum's been on them for forty years.
Jim Yes, she's not addicted to them, she just likes them.

A beat. Claire laughs

What are you laughing at?
Claire I was just thinking about that time we flew from Zurich.
Jim Which one was that?
Claire That was the time you called the air hostess over...
Jim I always call them over! That's what they're there for.
Claire Can you remember what you said? "I don't want to be alarmist but this wing is flapping up and down!" And she said, "When it stops flapping give me a shout".
Jim I'm sat there eyes glued on the bloody wing!
Claire For the rest of the flight you sat there with your face pressed on to the window, you had a blister on your forehead, can you remember? We've had some laughs, haven't we?

A beat

Jim Yes, most of them at my expense!

Jim and Claire find this amusing and share a laugh. They are extremely close here

Music

Fade Lights

Scene 5

Schiphol. Two days later, evening

There is a crash of thunder

Annie enters. She has a small backpack with her. She puts the backpack down and looks at her tickets

Dan, an older American Airlines pilot, crosses the stage. He has his flight bag with him and looks dashing

Annie Are you with KLM?
Dan Sorry?
Annie Am I at the right gate?
Dan Where are you going?
Annie Manchester.
Dan OK! The soccer team?
Annie That's right!
Dan Can I? (*He looks at her tickets*) OK, that looks like you're in the right place.
Annie Thanks.
Dan No problem. (*He hands the tickets back to Annie*)
Annie Where are you going?
Dan LAX.
Annie Oh right.
Dan You been?
Annie Hoping to.
Dan OK!
Annie Film school.
Dan Oh wow…

A silence as they both admire each other

Annie Is the flight delayed?
Dan Yours or mine?

Annie laughs more than she should

Annie Both.
Dan Do you fly much?
Annie Quite a bit. Do you?
Dan Well, I do, as it happens.
Annie I thought you might. (*She laughs more than she should*)
Dan Where are you from?
Annie Near Leeds?
Dan OK…
Annie Where are you from?
Dan I'm Australian!
Annie OK…
Dan Yeh…
Annie OK, you don't sound…

Dan I know…

Annie laughs

Annie Anyway, nice to meet you…
Dan And you … have a nice flight.
Annie And you…
Dan I will do… See you around!
Annie Well, you never know your luck.

Annie laughs and watches Dan go

Dan exits

Music

Fade Lights

Scene 6

Stuttgart. Two months later, night

Jim is C. *He is on the phone. He is dressed in a smart business suit. He has a small flight bag and a computer bag with him. He walks and talks animatedly. He looks very much the worse for a few business meetings. And has a small bottle of brandy with him*

Jim We're still in Stuttgart! No, Steve's gone to the bar. Pea soup here at the moment, … yes yes, so that's good. Might be here forever. I'd don't think they'll fly in this. … No, no, it's gone well. German rubber firm want a Health and Safety piece. Well, it's not Ghandi, is it? I said; it's not E.T. but it gets us a toe in the water! … I said it gets us a foot in the door. Can you hear me? Claire… Well, turn the radio off! There's somebody at the door… Well, I can't bloody answer it, can I? Listen love… I'll have to let you… Can you hear me? Can you hear me? I think she's gone. Can you hear me? I think she's gone. Can you hear me?

Steve enters. He too is on the mobile phone. He is dressed casually with an overnight bag and briefcase. He speaks unnecessarily loudly on the phone

Steve Sue, Sue, Sue, can you hear me?
Jim Everybody can hear you!

Steve Sue!

Jim They can hear you all over the bloody airport!

Steve Can you hear me? If you can hear me, I'll not be able to see you on Saturday. Man U have got Liverpool away. Can you hear me? ... Well, I never miss a match, you know that. ... Well, I'll go straight to Manchester, won't I? ... I always do... Listen, Sue, I'm losing you, I'll call you, let you know what's happening... Well, we're an hour delayed already so you never know ... OK...?

Jim Do you want one of these?

Steve (*into his phone*) Lost the signal...

Jim (*showing the bottles*) They're good, are these! I have one or two bottles in my pocket and I drink them during the flight. If I have two tablets and three brandies I'm nearly asleep on take off. I've got to time it right, though!

Steve You were a bit groggy in the meeting, weren't you? You couldn't speak.

Jim I'd mis-timed it because of the delay, I had to have another brandy. Usually a couple of coffees and I'm back on course, but...

Steve How did you think young Zoë got on?

Jim Handy on the German front! We've needed somebody like that for ages.

Steve Speaks three languages!

Jim I missed all that, all we did at school was learn to sing the French national anthem. Comes in handy if you're got the wrong seats at the rugby, but apart from that ... I hope this isn't going to be long!

Steve Yes, I've just had Sue going on about when will I see her again.

Jim Which is Sue?

Steve Ha ha.

Jim I can't keep track of your private life.

Steve So why do you keep asking me about it?

Jim To get an update.

Zoë enters. She is dressed in a smart suit, carries a bag and just about gets away with the image of a P.A. She brings a few chocolate buns with her

Zoë Bad news, I'm afraid!

Jim Oh, fuccckkinnn...

Zoë Another two hours.

Jim Here we go...

Steve Is that why we've got the buns?

Zoë It's all they had left. I thought a bit of chocolate might help.

Jim and Steve help themselves to the buns and eat

Jim Well, it's a start!

Zoë Well, I thought if we're hanging about.
Steve Good thinking. She's good, isn't she?
Zoë They reckon there's some bad weather coming over the channel.
Steve Don't tell Jim that, Zoë!
Zoë Oh sorry, I'm still learning. Is some information classified?
Steve We work on a need-to-know basis.
Jim And I don't need to know that!
Zoë I'll remember that!
Steve Mind you, he'll be pissed up on take off if he gets his timing right but this delay might throw him out of sequence.

We hear the bing-bong of the tannoy system. A German voice speaks

(*To Zoë*) What's she say?
Zoë Last call for the KLM flight to Malaga.

Steve moves to exit

Steve You fancy a drink, Jim? Zoë, can I get you a drink?
Zoë Is it OK?
Jim Yes, you two go and get sloshed at the bar, I'm stopping here.
Zoë Are you sure? You might be better with someone.
Jim No, no, I'm fine. I might even get on that Malaga flight.

Steve and Zoë turn to exit as Jim makes himself comfortable

We hear an aircraft overhead as Eva, a strikingly attractive East European hooker, enters. She smokes and has a drink

Eva You fly Manchester?
Jim Manchester.
Eva I come from Prague.
Jim Oh, right. Nice place.

A beat

Eva You have been?
Jim Some time ago!
Eva I go to Manchester.
Jim You fly a lot?
Eva Work all over.
Jim Well, I don't like flying, but it's a means to an end.

A beat

Eva You are alone?
Jim Me?
Eva You fly alone?
Jim My colleague's just popped to the bar...
Eva Ah, alone, uh?
Jim Well...

A beat

Eva In Manchester you can be mine host.
Jim Sorry?
Eva You can be mine host!
Jim Your host?
Eva For one night maybe.
Jim (*suddenly getting it*) Oh, right ... oh, well...
Eva I have good time if you like sexy.

A beat

Jim Eh? (*He laughs*)
Eva Why you laugh?
Jim I think you've got the wrong bloke.
Eva You no like to be mine host?
Jim Well...
Eva I will make you real good.
Jim No, listen...
Eva I have good flat.
Jim No, no, I'm married.

Eva laughs

Eva So?
Jim I've got a daughter, I'm happily married.
Eva Uh?
Jim Eh?
Eva Only man I've met says that!
Jim Well, there you go.
Eva I give gutt...
Jim No, no, chance, go on, go away.
Eva You come and be mine host for one night.
Jim Listen, I've got a mate, you should ask him.
Eva He like Manchester?
Jim Oh ay!

Eva I have gutt flat for him…

Jim walks around the departure lounge and laughs to himself

Jim Dear me!
Eva Why you laugh, you no like? You think I not make good host?
Jim Bloody hell…!
Eva I give good fuck in Manchester.
Jim Well, you should talk to my mate, then, he's Manchester mad!

Eva walks away from Jim as he laughs to himself. An aircraft is heard passing overhead

Zoë enters reading a magazine

So…
Zoë What?
Jim Everything OK…
Zoë Yeh.
Jim That's OK, then.

A beat

Zoë I've enjoyed it! I was a bit nervous at first; when you asked me, I wondered how it would work but…
Jim Steve's idea.
Zoë I wondered how you'd tracked me down?
Jim The travel firm.
Zoë I'd had enough of that.
Jim Well, I hope it works out.
Zoë So do I!

A beat

Jim Well, if I can ever be of any use…
Zoë Oh, great, thanks.
Jim I mean, I don't know everybody, but I've been around a bit so…
Zoë That's excellent, thanks a lot.
Jim I don't suppose you'll want to stay with us all your life.
Zoë Could be worse.
Jim It could be much worse.
Zoë Could be back in Benidorm.
Jim Don't knock it.

Zoë I wasn't!
Jim I don't mind young people going out and getting absolutely blasted in Spain and then make a nuisance of themselves on the plane on the way back. I stand by their right to do that!
Zoë As long as you're not on that flight?
Jim Got it in one!

A beat

So what did you do before, then?
Zoë I'd done a media course at Warwick University.
Jim Probably end up making films and laughing down at us, then?
Zoë Probably…
Jim I wouldn't be surprised, you've got the touch.
Zoë Have I?
Jim Oh ay.
Zoë Whatever that is!
Jim You ever heard of Bob Walker?
Zoë Film director, isn't he?
Jim I was at college with him. He used to say you get three chances, and if you don't take them, you're finished.
Zoë I think my problem is that I want it, but I want it now!
Jim Well, he got the chances, and I'm doing this! I don't regret it but… He was coming back from LA, Michael Douglas was on the flight, he had a script with him; showed it to Douglas, the next thing you know he's making a movie. He's made three in Hollywood.
Zoë And the moral is; take your chances.
Jim If that had been me I would never have even spoken to Michael Douglas.
Zoë Why not?

During the following, Steve enters upstage and watches them

Jim Frightened of rejection. I have been all my life! Funny because I've had so many you would have thought I'd be used to it by now, but…

She laughs at him easily

Zoë Oh.
Jim What?
Zoë You're funny!
Jim I know, but not funny ha ha! Eh?
Zoë No, you are, you make me laugh!
Jim Well, it's nice to know I'm good for something.

Zoë laughs even more at Jim. It is warm and bonding

Music

Fade Lights

Scene 7

Manchester. Three months later, day

Claire enters. She is dressed in summer wear and is looking forward to a few days in Cyprus. She is on the phone

Claire (*into the phone*) Mum, it's Claire, just letting you know we're at the airport. ... No, at the airport! ... No, we've not been anywhere yet, darling, we're going to Cyprus. ... Cyprus! ... Yes! ... No, I'm just letting you know that we're at the airport, because the traffic's been bad. There was an accident on the motorway, so... No, Mum, I'm at the airport, OK? ... See you later.

Jim enters. He is pushing a trolley which will not obey him

Jim I think the wheels have gone.
Claire Why we had to come over the top I don't know.
Jim There'd been a crash on the motorway.
Claire I don't know why we had to come over the moors?
Jim It was on the radio! I couldn't get around that tanker for an hour.
Claire Every time we get to the airport we have a bloody charade, and today because I'm churned up, you took your time getting here.
Jim What did you want me to do, drive under it?
Claire The trouble with you is you think you've got the monopoly on anxiety!
Jim Well, if you're anxious, let's not go.
Claire Oh, don't start that again!
Jim Because I can just as easily not go! I don't want to go to Cyprus anyway. I could just as easily not go, let you get on that plane and go home, that's the mood I'm in!
Claire Well, why don't you?

A beat

Jim What?
Claire Why don't you, because if you're going to be in that mood all holiday

I'd rather you not come, I don't know what's the matter with you. You've been like it this last two months.
Jim Well, I'll not come, then!

A beat

Claire What is wrong with you?
Jim It's not me, it's you.
Claire So what am I suppose to do?
Jim Go on your own if you want! I am not bothered about a week in Cyprus. I've got stuff to do anyway.
Claire It was a last minute bargain.
Jim I told you I couldn't really afford the time away from work but you still had to book it.
Claire Because you need a break.
Jim According to you!
Claire I can see what you're like!
Jim And I can see what you're like.
Claire Jesus! Why have you decided this now?
Jim I just have...
Claire Is it me, are you unhappy with me?
Jim I don't know what it is.
Claire So are you never flying again?
Jim I don't know...
Claire How are we going to see Annie again if you don't?
Jim I don't know.

Silence

Claire Right, then.
Jim What?
Claire Right! (*She pulls herself together and slowly wheels the trolley out of the departure lounge*)

Jim watches her in silence

Jim Where are you going?
Claire I'm going home... That's where I'm going, you've got your own way again.
Jim It's not about anybody getting their own way... It's about people being reasonable and telling me what you're planning for me!
Claire Oh, just forget it, will you!

Claire shunts the trolley off stage

Jim picks up the remaining bags and follows her off

Music

Fade Lights

Scene 8

Zaventum. Two weeks later, evening

Steve is talking to his girlfriend Sue on a mobile phone. He parades around the departure lounge

Steve Sue … you're not listening to me! I'm in Brussels… I know there's a problem with the washer, darling, but there isn't a lot I can do about it! Why didn't the man fix it? … Sue, honest, please, no, listen to me. Sue, I've been here before, darling, three times as it happens and it's not worth the aggro, honestly! Honestly! … So Craig's coming round to see to it, is he? Well, if you think you can deal with that, that's fine. I mean, think how I'll feel, we're seeing each other, the washer's leaking, I'm stuck in Brussels and you're getting your ex-husband to come around to fix it. I mean how would you feel? … I know there's water all over the kitchen, darling, you've told me that five times… Sue, I am now walking to board a plane to Manchester… Yes, it's all right … nice airport if you like that sort of thing…

Steve exits down one exit

Zoë enters from another. She too is on a mobile

Zoë Hi Jenny, it's Zoë, it's nine o'clock and I'm in Brussels. I'll call you when I get back! I was just ringing to say I'm looking forward to seeing you this weekend, love you, call me or text me. See you. Bye! (*She puts away her mobile*)

Jim enters. He is quite unkempt and carries two hot coffees

Jim An hour now, it said half an hour and that was forty minutes ago. So I've no idea what's going on.
Zoë I've bought you some little brandies, I thought you might…
Jim Oh, thanks…

Zoë No problem… (*She offers Jim a small bottle of brandy*)
Jim Steve got off?
Zoë Must have done, I saw him heading for the gate…
Jim Oh the phone as usual?
Zoë Manchester mad, isn't he?
Jim Never misses a match. He reckons they're one of the few things in this world that you can trust.
Zoë Manchester United?
Jim Puts a lot by them. Mind you, he goes through relationships like there's no tomorrow, so I suppose he's got to trust in something!

A beat

Zoë I can't work him out half the time.
Jim Good bloke. Completely opposite to me, I think that's why we get on. Nothing gets to him. He'd been married three times by the time he was forty.
Zoë Really?
Jim How he managed to make that work is beyond me. There was one time when he had three different women on the go and he wasn't married to any of them, and then there was his wife.
Zoë Why did he split up?
Jim Who with?
Zoë Well, any of them?
Jim You'll have to ask him.

A beat

Zoë My mum and dad split up when I was thirteen. I went well off the rails then.
Jim Oh dear…
Zoë Drugs…
Jim Oh dear.
Zoë Shagged about.
Jim Oh.
Zoë I don't know why they split up but…
Jim The grass is always greener, isn't it?
Zoë I dunno, is it?
Jim I dunno.
Zoë So they say!

A beat

Jim My parents have been together fifty-five years and never been unfaithful. They don't even speak to each other now, but at least they're together.

Zoë I think my dad started to play away... Mum was gutted but...

Jim I don't know what's the easiest, staying together after twenty years or splitting up.

Zoë Twenty years... That's nearly as long as I've been alive...

Jim Thanks for that!

Zoë I didn't mean it like that.

Jim I know you didn't, I'm joking.

Zoë stands and walks towards the fourth wall. Jim cannot help but watch her

Zoë It's starting to throw it down.

Jim I don't think I've ever flown in the clear blue sky. Mind you, when I'm above the clouds I don't feel too bad.

Zoë Like you haven't got as far to fall?

A beat

Jim I thought you were very good again today!

Zoë My French isn't quite as good as my German actually.

Jim My French is very poor. I can just about manage a cup of coffee and a ticket for the Metro!

Zoë Shall I go and see what's happening?

Jim No, no, I'll go.

Zoë It's not a problem.

Anita, a Belgian Service Air official, crosses the stage with a small cabin bag

Jim Here we are, look. Excuse 'em moi!

Anita Ar oui?

Jim Right, that's me done...

Zoë *A quelle heure l'avion departe a* Leeds/Bradford?

Anita *Il y a une faulte technicale.*

Zoë *Est-ce qu'il y a le possibilite le vol ne departerais pas*!

Anita *Oui, il y a le possibilite. Peutêtre une cancellation*!

Zoë Cancellation?

Anita It's possible!

Zoë *D'accord. Merci.*

Anita Bye! Bye!

Anita exits

Jim It's not cancelled, is it?
Zoë It could be.
Jim Is it cancelled or not?
Zoë I thought you didn't want to know?
Jim I want to know if it's cancelled!
Zoë Well, it could be…
Jim Oh, you're fuckkinnn…
Zoë There's a technical hitch!
Jim Oh, fuckinnn!
Zoë It's not definite!
Jim So what will they do, put another one on or what?
Zoë She didn't say! We could re-route to Schiphol or somewhere, I could see about that if you wanted?
Jim No!
Zoë I could go and have a look.
Jim Don't change routes.
Zoë OK.
Jim I can't do that!
Zoë OK.
Jim We're booked on this flight, let's stay on it!
Zoë OK.
Jim Whatever happens!
Zoë OK!
Jim I don't like changing things once we've made plans.
Zoë OK.
Jim I can't bear that!
Zoë Sorry.

Bing-bong of the tannoy, this time in French

Jim Here we go…

Zoë laughs

What are you laughing at?
Zoë You, you make me laugh!
Jim Well, that's good, then, isn't it!
Zoë Oh dear!
Jim 'Cause we could be here for days the way things are going!

Zoë laughs even more

Story of my life this… If ever I'm going somewhere there's always a problem. Usually it's me!

Zoë What about EuroStar? I could go and check!
Jim The cars at Leeds/Bradford though.
Zoë We could hire one.
Jim It's all extra cost, isn't it?
Zoë Just trying to help!

A beat

Jim Steve'll be watching Man United by now! I hope they get thrashed.
Zoë You're not a fan?
Jim I'm not a fan of anybody at the moment!

A beat

Zoë We could always go to a club and get them to phone us.
Jim Eh?
Zoë We could always go to a bar or something and get them to phone us, if you've had enough of waiting here!
Jim No ... we'll be all right here.
Zoë I just thought it could be more relaxing for you!
Jim A bar?
Zoë Or a club...
Jim No, I'm not...
Zoë Why not?
Jim Well...
Zoë Better than waiting here...

Anita enters

Jim and Zoë pay her some attention

Anita I am afraid it is not good for you. This flight for Leeds/Bradford is cancelled. It vill be tomorrow at six-thirty when they will make the flight...

A beat

Jim Oh great!
Zoë So what are we supposed to do?
Anita If you maybe go to the Novotel on the Grand Place and produce a receipt we will pay this, and also sort out for a taxi. All costs. It is a problem but... I will call for you a car.

Anita exits

Jim Bloody hell!

A beat

Zoë So it's a club, then?
Jim It could well be!
Zoë We'd better get to this hotel, I think there'll be a mad rush.
Jim I'd better phone Claire…

A beat

Zoë Do you think we'll have separate rooms?
Jim Well, I would have thought…
Zoë No, that's OK, then…
Jim Why?
Zoë I didn't want her to put us together and you get worried!
Jim No, people would talk.
Zoë Yes, right.
Jim Absolutely!
Zoë Because…
Jim What?
Zoë Well … you know…
Jim What?
Zoë Well, you know! I mean if you wanted to fuck me.

A beat

Jim What?
Zoë Nobody would know.
Jim Hey wow…
Zoë Just us…

A beat

Jim Hey…
Zoë What?
Jim Hey listen…
Zoë What?
Jim I'm one of the good blokes.
Zoë Sorry?

A beat

Jim I like to think of myself as one of the good blokes!

Zoë Meaning?
Jim Well…
Zoë What?
Jim I'm not going to take advantage.

A beat

Zoë Pity though.

A beat

Jim Yes but…
Zoë But what?

A beat

Jim I'm one of the good guys…
Zoë You said!
Jim I've got to keep telling myself.

A beat

Zoë I don't think there are many of you left.
Jim We're an endangered species!
Zoë Shame that!

A beat

Jim I do like you.
Zoë But not enough…
Jim Well…

A beat

Zoë Let's just forget it!

A beat

Jim You're … far too sexy for your own good.
Zoë Give up…
Jim Hey…
Zoë Now you're bullshitting.
Jim I'm not!
Zoë It's OK, I don't feel offended, don't worry about it!

Jim Eh?
Zoë Don't worry about it!
Jim Well, I'm not doing, but…
Zoë It's OK…

A beat

Jim When I tell Steve that we've got one night in Brussels all paid for and I didn't arrange it, he'll never believe me!
Zoë Don't tell him.
Jim No, that's right.

A beat

Zoë Anyway.
Jim I don't think it would be a smart thing to do…
Zoë OK…

A beat

Jim I mean me and Claire have had over twenty years…
Zoë You've said…
Jim And…
Zoë Like you said…

A beat

Jim I mean it's great to have one night but then what?
Zoë Forget it, I shouldn't have…
Jim Then it's meet the family and Sunday dinners!
Zoë Not yet!
Jim And then it's who shall we visit at Christmas and that's when all the trouble starts.
Zoë I don't fancy that.
Jim I really like you!
Zoë I like you!

Anita enters

Anita So I have a car … he will take you to the Novotel in Brussel, maybe you can have a meal, enjoy the nightlife and enjoy your stay in Brussel, uh?

Music

Fade Lights

Scene 9

Zaventem. Four days later, day

Jim is on stage. Steve is reading a paper. They are on a return flight. Jim is walking around trying to get a signal on his phone

Jim I'm trying to get hold of Claire, she's on about us going to Barcelona for a few days, next week. I don't know if I'm going to be free, the way this is going!
Steve Where's Zoë?
Jim She's trying to get an e-mail through to Jeff Steele in Birmingham about that Tesco's lark. (*Into the phone*) Claire? Can you hear me? She's got this thing about me relaxing more, I mean why she's booking these breaks is a mystery, it's just more stress! (*Into the phone*) I bet she's at the travel agents! Answermachine. Claire it's me. Don't book us that Barcelona thing, kid… I'm up to my neck in it. Over and out!

A beat

Steve Is Zoë all right, she seems a bit quiet today?

A beat

Jim Hey…
Steve What?
Jim Ohhh…
Steve What?
Jim We need to be careful there, you know?
Steve How do you mean?
Jim Oh!
Steve What?
Jim Well, I know what you would have done let's just say that.
Steve What?
Jim She's great, man, but bloody hell!
Steve What?
Jim Dangerous!
Steve How's this, then?
Jim I mean she's great but…
Steve What happened?
Jim Well, we went for an Indonesian and that was it! I had a gippy stomach the next day and all.
Steve I thought you hated spicy food?

Jim I do but the whole thing threw me! Hey don't, because, you know… I mean she's a lovely lass but…
Steve Did she, erm?
Jim Made it very clear, let's just say that! Said I could, you know, if I wanted…
Steve (*enjoying it*) Oh oh!
Jim Oh yes!

A beat

Steve So what's the problem?
Jim She's twenty years too fucking late, mate, that's the problem!
Steve Oh oh!

A beat

Jim It's the last thing I want.
Steve You like her, though, don't you?
Jim Course I do.
Steve Well…
Jim Wow hey…
Steve Man… Oh hey…

A beat

Jim I told Claire about what happened, so…
Steve What, about her coming on?
Jim What do you think I am?
Steve I was going to say.
Jim About us staying in the same hotel!
Steve And she believed nothing happened?
Jim Nothing did happen!
Steve Well, I wouldn't have even told her that.
Jim Why not?
Steve 'Cause it looks like something happened!
Jim Like what?
Steve Like you're covering, by telling her nothing happened.
Jim Nothing did!
Steve Therefore there's nothing to tell!
Jim Steve, I told her nothing happened, because nothing happened!
Steve Yes, but you telling her that nothing happened looks like something happened.
Jim No, it doesn't, does it?

Steve Well, I never told any of mine things like that.
Jim No, because with you something usually happens! Doesn't it?
Steve Well, ay!

A beat

Jim No, you know, it would have been nice and all that but…
Steve Well, there you go, that's your chance gone!
Jim (*philosophically*) I couldn't believe it…
Steve I don't know why you didn't take her up on her offer?
Jim Because I'm a King, Steve!
Steve You must be…

A beat

Jim And I'll tell you, it's hard work being a King…
Steve Well, I'm not a King.
Jim I know that!
Steve I'm a pauper with three kids to feed…
Jim You've got three of bloody everything, haven't you?

A beat

Steve She must have been a bit shocked!
Jim What?
Steve When you turned her down.
Jim I did it for her own good.
Steve Did you tell her that?
Jim And I did it for Claire, I did it for the company, and I did it for you and all!
Steve You could have knobbed her senseless for me.

A beat

Jim I'd've probably had a heart attack, the stress I'm under.
Steve That would have been a bit awkward to explain.

A beat

Jim Why does it always happen to me? I mean, seven months ago a woman offered me sex in Stuttgart airport.
Steve Well, you kept that quiet.
Jim When we went to Prague I was the only one who got accosted! Three

times! Twice in the street and once, at a service station, nice and all, stood there in the middle of nowhere, wearing a bikini and holding a bloody towel. I mean what is it about my face?
Steve People just want to sit on it!

Jim laughs and gets his mobile out once more

Jim Yeh, well, don't you get any ideas! I'll try Claire again, if she books this Barcelona thing, I'll go through the bloody roof.

Music

Fade Lights

Scene 10

Manchester. A week later, evening

Claire sits in Departures, she is reading. Jim is standing by the fourth wall having a drink

Jim Four days in Barcelona, then.

A beat

And when's this Dallas thing, then?
Claire Whenever Annie can hook up with Dan.
Jim Bloody Dallas!
Claire It's the nearest place to meet, he's on a long haul and she says she'll just hop over.
Jim Hop over? Goor, Annie, she's even bought the jargon!
Claire I've always fancied going to Dallas. All that Kennedy stuff.
Jim Well, it does nothing for me!
Claire Fascinating.

A beat

Jim She met him at an airport, then?
Claire Amsterdam!
Jim Bloody hell!
Claire He tries to arrange his flights around her.
Jim It'll never last, will it…

Claire How do you know?
Jim Oh, come on?
Claire I think that's romantic!
Jim They don't even know each other.
Claire Well, they'll find out, won't they?

A beat

Jim Oh dear Annie!
Claire Look at us, we know everything about each other, that's not necessarily a good recipe, is it?

A beat

Jim I met you at a Bowie concert in Bradford! That's a bit different to meeting at Schiphol airport. Mind you I've been to Schiphol, there was probably as much eye make-up...

A beat

Claire She says he's a nice guy...
Jim Mr Nice guy!
Claire A bit older but...
Jim What?
Claire She says he's a bit older.
Jim How much older?
Claire A bit!
Jim What is he, a war veteran?
Claire He's just older.
Jim Just older or a bit older?
Claire She didn't say!
Jim A bit older?
Claire Yes, like you.

A beat

Jim Well, if he is older it'll save us the joy of meeting the parents.
Claire Not necessarily!
Jim With a bit of luck they might even be dead! That'll save all the arguments at the wedding.
Claire I don't think it's that serious.

Jim starts to move around the Departure lounge

Jim You know, I bet everybody has a case of the jitters, when they come to an airport. You look at half of them and they aren't actually reading. They've got the book in front of them but they don't really know what they're reading.

Claire Well, I do!

Jim What have you just read, then?

Claire I can't read for you going on…

Jim That's why airport novels are so thick, it's not because they're about anything grandiose, it's because the authors know that the reader has forgotten what he's read almost as soon as he's read it. So they have to repeat it three times because it'll not go in, because everyone who's reading is just thinking, "shit, I hope the plane doesn't crash"!

Claire Not everybody's like you!

Jim We were in Brussels last month, and there's this guy sat there reading the *Financial Times*, only he's got the paper upside down.

Claire He must have been Australian!

Jim I'll tell you something else! Do you think the air hostesses ever get frightened?

Claire I am reading this, actually.

Jim They wear far too much face make-up for my liking… Do you know why? That's because their faces are completely covered in wrinkles from years of thinking "bollocks, this is it"!

Claire You should write some of this down.

Silence

Jim Four days in Barcelona, then, doing nothing.

Claire You can do what you want.

Jim I will do.

Claire You always do!

A beat

Jim Maybe I'll just go off…

Claire Go off with Zoë, then. Why don't you call her or send her a text message, isn't that the new love letter?

Jim I don't know where you've got this thing about Zoë from?

Claire I'm sure she'll want to stay in another nice hotel.

A beat

Jim I could have had a hundred Zoës!

Claire Oh, don't kid yourself.

Jim Why do you think I couldn't?
Claire You're in danger of believing your own bullshit, did you know that?
Jim Yes, very good, Claire, very cutting.
Claire And that'd make you feel younger, would it? Having a hundred Zoës?
Jim Well, a hundred might be pushing it a bit, but…
Claire What do you think they'll be after, your body or your money?
Jim Either, I'm not bothered!

A beat

Claire You daren't get on a plane without a drink, Jim, so the idea of you shagging your way around Europe is pushing it a bit, don't you think?
Jim Do you think so?
Claire I know you, you couldn't live with yourself.
Jim Yeh, well…
Claire You're not Steve, are you?
Jim Meaning what?
Claire Well…
Jim What's wrong, do you want me to be?
Claire You couldn't have an affair, you haven't got time for me and Annie, how are you going to find time to have a bloody affair?
Jim I could find time.
Claire So are you saying that's what you want?
Jim Well, I don't want this!
Claire Do you think I do?
Jim This is just pointless to me!
Claire Oh, life's too short!
Jim Exactly.
Claire Do what you want, honestly…

A beat

Jim Men and women, look at us! We're not made for each other, are we?
Claire You'd know!
Jim Well, a woman's at her sexual peak at thirty-five and a man's at his at seventeen! Now who the bloody hell thought that up? That's just bad planning!
Claire It might be for you.
Jim Well, come on!
Claire It sounds just about right for me!

A beat

Jim Well, you know what to do, then, don't you?

Claire Well, you're twenty-five years past your sell-by date, so I can't see many people rushing to get you off the shelf! You'll just be stuck there like a can of mouldy beans! (*She begins to laugh to herself*)

Jim looks at her. She laughs quite heartily and freely

Jim I'll go and get another drink, do you want one?
Claire Ay, get me a bloody big brandy!

Music

Fade Lights

Scene 11

Schiphol. A month later, night

Zoë is in Departures, she speaks on her mobile phone. She is very enthusiastic, effusive and excitable

Zoë (*into the phone*) Hiya, it's Zoë, I'm in Amsterdam! ... Yes, yes! It's OK, a bit samey. Well, you don't see much, mostly airports. ... I don't know, I mean it's OK at the moment but... But I'm not going to be with them forever! ... I dunno, you never know, do you... I'll be back in London next month so we can... Well, anything really! Telly! Fashion! You know me, I'll give anything a go! Listen, it's a bad line ... the weather's... Jenny? (*She puts the phone away*)

Jim enters. He is dressed in a casual suit, and is more unkempt than we have seen him before. He carries two coffees

Jim The weather's not getting any better! Coffee?
Zoë They're having to put another plane on, there's a problem with the regular one apparently, I'm going to pop back and see what's what...
Jim Don't tell me about changes...
Zoë I'm just warning you.
Jim (*joking*) Don't do it to me!
Zoë I thought you needed to know.
Jim I don't need to know anything like that.
Zoë I'll go and see what's what in a minute.

Both sip at their coffee

Jim So that's been a good day!
Zoë A very good day!
Jim Told you, didn't I?
Zoë What?
Jim We could be mates.
Zoë Absolutely.
Jim That's right.
Zoë Great!

A beat

Jim I did all that years or so ago, you know?
Zoë All what?
Jim I've been about a bit...
Zoë You keep saying that...
Jim Well...
Zoë I believe you, don't worry. You don't have to keep saying it.
Jim I'm not doing, am I?
Zoë I thought you said to forget it!
Jim I did, I have. (*He looks at Zoë, it is too long and meaningful*) Anyway.
Zoë What?
Jim Nothing.

Zoë goes to move

Where are you going?
Zoë I'm going to the prayer room.
Jim Really?
Zoë No, I'm joking...
Jim Well, I always go!
Zoë I know that, I was pulling your leg.
Jim Hey, I am the boss, you know...
Zoë Sorry, sir! I'll go and see what's happening.
Jim Sit down, relax.
Zoë It's my job...

Zoë exits

Jim laughs, and reclines

Steve enters. He is reading a paper and eating a chocolate bun

Steve Two tickets for the final, you coming?

Jim What's happened to Sue, doesn't she want to go?
Steve No, that's all gone a bit…
Jim Tits up?
Steve I don't understand her and all that!
Jim Oh, that one!
Steve There's too much baggage there anyway. I think the husband's coming back. It was all getting a bit messy, so…
Jim Haven't you got anybody lined up?
Steve Not yet!
Jim Slacking, aren't you?
Steve It's early days yet!

Jim stands and wanders around the departure lounge. He settles on looking out into the night

Jim I was just wondering how we got into all this? It sounded great at the time, didn't it? Set up a business, fly around the world…
Steve Meet interesting and exciting people…
Jim And try to shag some of them?
Steve Unfair!
Jim That's your mission statement, isn't it?
Steve What do you want to do, go back to schlepping up and down the motorway, selling menus?

Jim looks out into the night

Jim It's pissing it down out here again.
Steve We should be all right. We're on the Frankfurt express, aren't we?
Jim Zoë says they're changing it.
Steve Well, it was out there half an hour ago.
Jim Well, all I can see is this little one with a propeller.
Steve Oh, you're joking! (*He stands up and comes downstage to the side of Jim*)
Jim Well, that's all there is out here.
Steve That's not the Frankfurt express.
Jim No, I didn't think it was.
Steve That's a bit small, isn't it?
Jim Look at it!
Steve There's only one step up to it.
Jim I thought you'd fly on anything?
Steve Yes, but that's beyond a bloody joke that is!
Jim Look at the bloody weather and all.

Zoë enters and grabs her bags

Zoë I think they're ready, we can start boarding.
Jim Well, that'll not take long, it only holds four.
Steve What gate are we boarding from?
Zoë We're just down here! (*She gestures* DR)
Steve Right, I'll go and help the pilot wind it up… It's the first time I've felt nervous… You haven't got any of them bottles of brandy left, have you?
Jim I've just drank the last one, kid.
Steve (*going*) Now I know how you feel.

Steve grabs his belongings and exits

A beat

Zoë stays with Jim

Zoë Are you going to be all right on that?
Jim Oh ay, no problem.
Zoë Are you sure? (*She turns to go*)
Jim Well, you'll hold me hand, won't you?
Zoë If you want.
Jim Would you?
Zoë If you want.
Jim Give us a hug.

Zoë hugs Jim. It is very affectionate

Mmmm!
Zoë All right?
Jim I'm all right, it's Steve you should worry about.
Zoë I'll save you a window seat! (*She is almost off stage*)
Jim Yes, so I can see the wings flapping!
Zoë You what?
Jim I'm joking!
Zoë Oh, you get me every time.
Jim (*half to himself*) I'm just joking.

Zoë exits

Jim goes to his belongings, opens his bag and takes a few tablets. He then takes out a small bottle of brandy from his jacket pocket. And downs one bottle. We hear the bing-bong of the airport tannoy

Sorry, Steve, mate!

Jim downs another brandy and walks purposefully towards the plane

Music

Fade Lights

CURTAIN

ACT II

Scene 1

Prague. A month later, evening

Lights come up on Eva sitting at the coffee table. She has a plastic coffee cup with her. She is eyeing up Zoë who is sitting playing with her mobile

A number of announcements are made over the tannoy. Neither Zoë nor Eva can make any sense of the announcements. They shake their heads at each other as Zoë begins to speak into her phone

Zoë (*into the phone*) Jenny, it's Zoë! I thought I'd catch you, you're probably back at work! Did you get the flowers? I'm in Prague at the moment! I just wanted to let you know that I've got an interview at Granada TV in Manchester. I can't remember if I told you or not! Anyway, it's next month, so fingers crossed! Flying back to Leeds/Bradford via Amsterdam, and at the moment we're only delayed fifty minutes. Talk soon! (*She puts away her phone and looks out towards the fourth wall*)
Eva Rain!
Zoë Again!
Eva You like?
Zoë Prague?
Eva You like?
Zoë What I've seen of it!
Eva Beautiful city, but very dangerous!
Zoë Really?
Eva (*shaking her hand*) Hooowww!
Zoë Really?

A beat

Eva I fly to Manchester.
Zoë Very different.
Eva Yes, but I like...

A beat

You are alone?
Zoë Me?
Eva You are alone?
Zoë No, my colleagues are at the bar. I couldn't get a signal so…

A beat

Eva You work in Manchester?
Zoë No… I erm…
Eva Sorry, I hear…
Zoë Oh, no, I'm applying for a job there!
Eva Ah secret uh…
Zoë Well…

We hear the bing-bong announcing a flight in German

Eva In Manchester, I have flat.
Zoë Really?
Eva You ever in Manchester?
Zoë Maybe!
Eva We meet.
Zoë Well…
Eva Have drink!
Zoë Yes?
Eva Maybe have good time?
Zoë Well?
Eva I have good flat in Manchester. You like we meet in Manchester?
Zoë Well?
Eva I give you number… You call me in Manchester… (*She gives Zoë a piece of paper with a number on it*) You in Manchester, you call me, OK?
Zoë Well, you never know!

Steve enters. He is speaking into the phone

Eva exits

Steve comes downstage and looks at the weather. Zoë sits and reads

Steve (*into the phone*) Yes! Hang on, I've got you now. I was up at the bar, there's no… No, it's last call for me… Barcelona.
Zoë Seen the weather?
Steve Hallo?
Zoë Fifty minutes delayed, mine!

Steve twists and turns to get a signal

Steve I thought you said it was over?
Zoë I'm going to get a magazine.
Steve I thought he'd come back?

Zoë exits

Steve stands and speaks into the phone. He is agitated

I know he only came to fix the washer, darling, that's what they all say! Well, you should have thought about that before he got his plumbing tackle out! … It was a joke… I know it's not the right time for a…! … Well, I thought I could trust you! I know you've been married to him for a long time but… I am trying to support you… Well, I'm here talking to you… Sue… I'm losing you… I'm losing you… I'll call you back when I get a better signal! (*He takes his mobile away from his ear so he cannot hear*)

Jim enters, carrying a briefcase and a flight bag. And looking at his mobile phone. He looks at Steve

I've lost her!
Jim You can call her back on this if you want?
Steve No, I'll…

Jim looks at the weather

Jim You seen the weather?
Steve Keeps ringing me.
Jim I thought the husband was back?
Steve He is, but she's texting me, telling me what she wants to do to me! And now she's on about us meeting up tomorrow to sort it out. Well, I'll be at the final tomorrow, so if she wants to get down to Spain fair enough!
Jim I don't know how you do it.
Steve I dunno, it's just a game, mate.
Jim A game of two halves?
Steve I think it's all over.

Jim looks out towards the rain

Jim I say the weather's a bit…?
Steve I'm not bothered as long as it's not another one of those little 'uns.
Jim I didn't mind that one. They don't go up as high.

Steve You were pissed senseless, weren't you? You could have been sat on the tail and it wouldn't have bothered you! (*He feels for his tickets and prepares to depart*)
Jim It's heavy-going out here, isn't it?
Steve Hard-nosed bastards!
Jim It's business, Jim, but not as we know it.
Steve I'm back on Thursday, then! Listen, I'm going to have to make a move.
Jim I'll call you.
Steve Don't text me, I might get the wrong idea!

Steve exits in haste

Jim sits, and looks at a magazine he has in his briefcase

Zoë enters; she has a magazine with her

Zoë He gone?
Jim Just!
Zoë Didn't you want to go with him?
Jim No, football doesn't do a lot for me, to be honest.
Zoë Didn't you ever play?
Jim Oh ay, I played. I played for the Boys Brigade as a kid! I fancied myself as a goalie. But after I let nineteen goals in and my dad had left the pitch in disgust and public humiliation, I thought better of it. I started playing solitaire after that.

Zoë laughs at him

Zoë Oh, don't!
Jim What?
Zoë Set me off laughing again.
Jim I'm not.
Zoë Every time you open your mouth, I'm laughing.

A beat

Jim Did I tell you when I was involved in a near miss?
Zoë No.
Jim Oh ay!
Zoë Really?
Jim Straight up!
Zoë You always say that!
Jim Honestly! The first time I flew. That's why I'm like I am now. I went

up with this mate. He was sat there all relaxed and I said to him, "See that!" and he says "What?" I said; another aircraft just went past us! He said "Where?" I says, "Just out here". I was sat by the window! He says "You lying bastard!" I said "No way, I even saw the pilot, he winked at me!" It was here, about twenty yards away!

Zoë Really?

Jim I saw the pilot, we were that close! We were that close, I could see his fillings. Listen, we were that close I recognized him.

Zoë Really?

Jim I went to school with him!

Zoë Oh yes?

Jim I always keep an eye on the air hostesses now, do you?

Zoë No.

Jim No?

Zoë No.

Jim You're a freak!

Zoë I'm not...

Jim Everybody keeps their eyes on the air hostesses during the flight, especially on take off. The merest blink to each other and that's me putting a life jacket on.

Zoë Give up.

Jim I'm serious! If the bing-bong thing goes and they look at each other, that's bad! I think we're going down, I mean it probably it means they've run out of Chanel Number Five, but to me...

Zoë Have you ever been up into the cockpit.

Jim Yes.

Zoë Didn't that make you feel any better?

Jim No.

Zoë Why not?

Jim Well, I mean where's the white line?

Zoë Stop it!

Jim Where's the cat's eyes?

Zoë They're down there somewhere.

Jim It's just blue out in front of you. I mean, half the time they're not even flying the bloody thing... No, I mean I get on... But, if they could put me in a crate and add water and mix at the other end I'd be a lot better. And when it banks, I'm holding on... I expect it to turn upside down. Steve said he'd been on one that did that once... That'd be it for me, I'd never fly again! And what's all this about the mile high club?

Zoë You're not a member, then?

Jim Well, I've no chance.

Zoë Oh, why not?

Jim Well, you've seen me, I don't stand up, so there's not a lot of chance of anything else happening!

A beat

Zoë Oh, dear.
Jim I'm not joking, you know.
Zoë I know, I believe you. Thousands wouldn't.
Jim Always happens to me!

A beat

Zoë I think you're in the wrong job.
Jim The wrong job or the wrong life?
Zoë Which?

A beat

Jim Are you flirting with me?
Zoë Are you flirting with me?
Jim Erm…?
Zoë Erm…?
Jim Erm, yes, I am flirting with you!
Zoë OK.
Jim That's OK, isn't it?
Zoë It's fine.

A beat

Jim I kind of hoped you'd got that, you know?
Zoë What?
Jim That I was flirting with you!
Zoë I just needed for it to be made official.

A beat

Jim It's a long way from Benidorm, Zoë!
Zoë It is.
Jim Look at us in Prague.
Zoë Jet-setters!

A beat

Jim Steve's idea!
Zoë Good old Steve!

A beat

Jim Yes, I think he had his eye on you.
Zoë I think he did.
Jim Right from when we got on the bus at the airport.
Zoë I could see that!
Jim What is he like?

A beat

Zoë Well, he didn't get very far!
Jim He tried, then?
Zoë Oh!
Jim When?
Zoë One night on the beach. It was early on. I think he said you had a meeting.
Jim With the bloke from the Town Hall?
Zoë I think that was it.
Jim He set that meeting up.

A beat

Zoë Well, he didn't get very far.
Jim How far did he get?
Zoë Eh?
Jim How far did he get, then?
Zoë Not very far.

A beat

Jim And what does that mean?
Zoë He didn't get very far.

A beat

Jim Did he get kissing far?
Zoë What?
Jim Did he get kissing far?

A beat

Zoë Yes, he got kissing far.
Jim Oh, right!
Zoë But you know…
Jim What?
Zoë Not much further.

A beat

Jim I can't believe he'd even try it on, we were supposed to be fucking working!

A beat

Zoë Well, he didn't get very much further after that.

A beat

Jim How much further did he get after that, then?
Zoë What?
Jim How far after that did he get?
Zoë I can't tell you that.

A beat

Jim So he got a lot further than you're telling me?
Zoë No!
Jim Come on…?
Zoë He didn't.

A beat

Jim I've known him a long time. I know what he's like!
Zoë Well, anyway.
Jim I bet he wanted to…
Zoë I thought we were mates?
Jim We are…
Zoë Well, as a mate, forget it, all right?

A beat

Jim So Steve tried, but he didn't get very far…
Zoë No!
Jim Ha ha!
Zoë What?
Jim He's a sad bastard!

A beat

Zoë Dallas next week?

Jim Dallas! I can't wait; another eleven hours stuck in the sky in a tin can. I don't know why I don't lose more weight.
Zoë Sounds great!
Jim The amount of flying I do, I should only weigh about three stone.
Zoë I've always been fascinated by the Kennedys. Always wanted to go that place where they shot him...
Jim You're morbid you are.
Zoë I'm not.
Jim You like flying, and want to see where a bloke was shot through the neck. Come on.
Zoë You should have a good time.
Jim Ten days in Dallas? I might learn line dancing!
Zoë Bring me something back.
Jim I'll bring you a steak back. How do you like it served?
Zoë Just cut its horns off and wipe its arse.
Jim Oh yes, very good!
Zoë Funny?
Jim Very nearly!

Jim and Zoë laugh together

Music

Fade Lights

SCENE 2

Edinburgh. Four days later, day

Steve enters with an overnight bag and a briefcase. He is on the mobile phone

Steve (*into the phone*) Sue ... listen... No, I'm in Edinburgh. Well, I think what I'm saying is that it's all over bar the shouting! That it's all over... You're breaking up, love. No, I said... I think it's full time...

Jim enters, he too is on the phone

Jim Zoë, it's Jim! Can you fax the "selling smart" stuff through to Colin Ward in Edinburgh again?
Steve (*to Jim*) It's full time here, but Sue wants to play on.
Jim ...and also send him a hard copy. He's being a bit of an arse about the fax. And double check those Dallas tickets for me, will you? ... I've got to have extra leg room. If I'm cooped up like a pigeon I'll cluck! All right, kid, see you.

Steve (*to Jim*) Sue. I think we need to bring a sub on!

Jim snaps away his phone

Jim You can see her one more time, can't you?
Steve I can't, I know what'll happen and then it'll all kick off again! I want to hang up my boots!

A beat

Jim You know about the Belgian meeting, don't you?
Steve Don't trust me, do you?
Jim I'm just gently reminding you. It's when we're in Dallas! I don't want to come back and discover we've missed it! Zoë's got all the details, so…
Steve Well, she'll come with me, won't she?
Jim Eh?
Steve She'll come with me.
Jim No!
Steve She is.

A beat

Jim She's not.
Steve I thought she was.
Jim I don't think she needs to.
Steve Eh?
Jim I mean she doesn't need to, does she?
Steve Oh, right!

A beat

Jim Why, do you need her?
Steve Well, it could be handy on the French front. I mean my French is worse than yours.
Jim Oh, right.
Steve I mean if you want me to come back with a contract and not just two pints of Stella, it could be useful!
Jim Oh, right!
Steve I mean if you don't mind sharing her out.
Jim Ha ha!
Steve Bloody hell!
Jim What?
Steve Don't leave me without any back-up in Brussels, man!

A beat

Jim I just didn't think she needed to, that's all.
Steve Well, I mean…?
Jim Sorry, mate!
Steve Make me look a right arse without somebody.

A beat

Jim No, no, you're right.
Steve I mean, I know you're close but…
Jim Sorry, mate!
Steve I mean, if I could manage without her, I would do, but…
Jim No, no, fair enough!
Steve I know every time she comes out it's another three hundred quid but I think this is justified.
Jim Meaning?
Steve Every time she's been out with us, it's an extra three hundred quid.
Jim And what?
Steve Well…
Jim What?
Steve Well, we could have managed in Amsterdam, couldn't we? They all speak English.
Jim It was just a little jolly, man.
Steve I know what it was!
Jim It was just a perk!
Steve I mean, she can't speak Czech but she came to Prague, didn't she?
Jim (*defensively*) Bloody hell, Steve…
Steve I'm not saying it's wrong but…

A beat

Jim What's up, do you miss my company?
Steve Well, I do as it happens but…

A bing-bong in English. The men start to move

Jim (*to the tannoy*) Oh, here we go…
Steve Well, I'm complicit, aren't I?
Jim Eh?
Steve I'm complicit whenever I meet Claire!
Jim Well, I would have thought given your track record that a platonic friendship was fairly easy to keep quiet about?
Steve I'm only saying what others are thinking.

Jim Nothing's happening!
Steve Nothing physical!
Jim Hey man…
Steve Does Claire know?
Jim About what?
Steve About this platonic…
Jim She knows we have a relationship…
Steve Does she?
Jim I've told her all about her…
Steve Ohh!
Jim What?
Steve You're torturing her!
Jim Bollocks!
Steve Tell 'em nothing.
Jim Oh dear!
Steve You're talking to an expert here.
Jim You're still in the swamp, mate! It's OK to like somebody, you know! We've moved on, Steve.
Steve Have we?

A beat

Jim Anyway, look, there isn't a problem, she can go with you. I'll give her a call when you're there, just to see how you've got on.
Steve What do you think I'm going to do?
Jim I like her, Steve.
Steve I know you do!
Jim I do really like her.

Steve is teasing. They are walking to the gate

Steve You know what, though, don't you?
Jim I do like her!
Steve Ha ha!
Jim What?
Steve You're married, though, mate!
Jim I know!

Both men laugh at each other as they exit. But Jim is uneasy

Music

Fade Lights

Scene 3

Heathrow. A week later, day

Claire is on stage, dressed quite smartly, and is checking her boarding cards with Alison, a young woman who works for American Airways. The two of them are studying the cards

Claire Well, we did book it!
Alison I'm sorry, but there's nothing I can do.
Claire We did book!
Alison I'm sorry.
Claire I phoned up and the woman said we'd get extra leg room.
Alison Well, I'm sorry.
Claire She said they'd put us in an emergency seat. And according to the girl at check-in we're at the back, my husband's going mad.
Alison I'm sorry, there's nothing I can do. These seats are quite down the plane, there's quite a bit of room.
Claire Well, we did phone up, and the girl said we'd be able to reserve extra leg room, and that's what we thought we'd done, and before we knew it we'd been issued these tickets. You see, my husband isn't the best flyer…
Alison I'm sorry, but the only seats with extra leg room are on the bulk head or at the emergency seats. Is your husband disabled at all?
Claire No, but somebody will be if he's stuck at the back for eleven hours.
Alison I'm sorry…
Claire This is a recipe for air rage, I can tell you.
Alison Well, I'll go and see what I can do, but I can't promise anything.

Alison exits

Claire sits with her belongings and is growing increasingly anxious

Jim enters after a while

Jim No bloody joy, they just smile at me like I'm backward.
Claire She says she'll go and see, but…
Jim Bloody great!
Claire The woman said we'd be able to get extra room.
Jim Cooped up for a day!
Claire Zoë said we could reserve the seats.
Jim No wonder my nerves are shot by the time I get on the plane, we have to go through this charade every time we check in.

A beat

Claire Annie says that when we get in we'll have an hour before Dan has to go to a meeting.
Jim All that way for an hour! That's barmy and all.
Claire We'll be all right once we get there.
Jim I don't know why we have to go for ten days?
Claire Well, there's a lot to see! I think she wants to look around there anyway! She says we could go to Fort Worth. It's a cowboy town.
Jim Yee har!

A beat

So we're going to just meet him for an hour in the airport, then?
Claire I've just said that.
Jim And we're to glean all about a future member of our family from that viewing, are we?
Claire We'll meet Dan and then go to the Marriott, they've booked us into one nearby.

A beat

Jim Where's she getting the money from?
Claire Dan's paying.
Jim I don't know if I like that so much, the boyfriend paying?
Claire Well, I did say that you'd pay but ... Dan insisted.
Jim Be on a fair whack anyway, won't he?
Claire I've no idea.
Jim Be ready for retiring soon and all. That'll be another hand-out.
Claire I don't think he's that old.

A beat

Jim How's she getting on in LA, has she said?
Claire She says it's bullshit central, but you know Annie, she just drifts along on an even keel, nothing seems to get to her.
Jim A chip off the old block.
Claire Well?
Jim She gets that from me.
Claire Oh, yes?
Jim She does, I'm easy going, me.
Claire Are you hell!
Jim Well, you aren't, you're pent-up all the bloody time, you are.
Claire I am when I'm at the airport with you.
Jim Hey listen, I could just as easy not go, get on the Brussels flight, there's plenty I could do.

Claire Ten days in Dallas with you in this mood! Absolutely bloody great!
Jim Yee har!

A beat

Claire I hope somebody shoots you!

Music

Fade Lights

Scene 4

Dallas. Two days later, day

Annie, Jim, Claire and Dan are all on stage. They shake hands as they are introduced in the following scene

Annie This is my mum…
Claire Hallo.
Annie This is my dad.
Jim Hallo there…
Annie This is Dan…
Claire I think we'd got that…
Dan Hallo…
Jim Hallo, mate, how are you?
Dan I'm fine, thanks…

Silence

Jim Good. Good. That's good, then…
Claire Well, here we are!

The four of them laugh through the awkwardness

Jim Yee har!

Music

Fade Lights

Scene 5

Dallas Forth Worth. Five minutes later, day

Annie, Dan, Claire and Jim are standing in slightly different positions. They are still laughing as we meet them

Dan Annie says you're not a great flyer?

Everyone laughs, except Jim, at his expense

Jim What's so funny about that?

They laugh again

Annie Dan meant it as a joke, Dad...
Claire He does OK, don't you?
Jim That's right.

They laugh again

Dan Well, at least you're here...
Jim We've got to go back, though!
Dan That's right.
Jim Back to reality!
Annie OK, let's do Dallas!

They laugh again

Music

Fade Lights

Scene 6

Dallas Forth Worth. Ten days later, evening

Annie, Dan, Claire and Jim are wearing the same clothes but they are standing in slightly different positions on stage

Jim Well, anyway.
Dan Been a real pleasure, sir!

They shake hands

Claire Lovely to meet you!

Claire shakes hands with Dan. Dan pecks her

Dan Take care, Claire.
Claire I will do...
Dan And don't worry about Annie, she's doing great.
Jim Yep...
Annie See you, Dad... (*She hugs Jim*)
Dan Yeh, see you, Dad. (*He hugs Jim*)
Jim Missing you already!
Annie What is he like?
Jim See you, kid!
Annie And don't worry ... just get on that plane...
Jim Not a lot else I can do, is there?

Annie hugs Jim. Claire pecks Dan. Claire hugs Annie

Music

Fade Lights

Scene 7

Dallas Fort Worth. Three hours later, evening

Jim and Claire are alone on stage. Claire has a number of posh carrier bags with her, they also have their hand luggage

Claire Well, there we are, then, ten days in Dallas...
Jim Didn't see a lot of Dan, though, did we?

A beat

Claire Well, anyway, I thought he was a nice guy.
Jim Mr Nice Guy...
Claire Please!
Jim "Hi, my name's Dan, I'm a nice guy. I smile all the time and I seem completely one-dimensional!"
Claire Christ...

Jim "I'm fifty-five years old and I'm going to make Annie very happy here in the US!"
Claire He's not fifty-five!
Jim Completely false.
Claire His hair wasn't.
Jim His smile was!
Claire Here we go.
Jim Plastic.
Claire Give up!

A beat

Jim I'll tell you something else, I don't think he knows as much about flying as I do.
Claire No, he loved it when you were telling him how to land a jumbo, didn't he? You could see his smile wilting!

A beat

Jim I mean, we still don't know anything about him, do we?
Claire Smart though!
Jim It's the uniform, isn't it?
Claire I thought he looked well turned out.
Jim He's as old as I am!
Claire Looks like he looks after himself…
Jim I bet he's fifty-five.
Claire Well, I thought he looked fit.
Jim Oh ay!
Claire He happens to look like a big smart fit bloke, and Annie obviously likes him, so…

A beat

Jim She's only a bit of a kid.
Claire She knows what she's doing.
Jim Does she?
Claire Well, she'll find out, won't she.
Jim Find out what?
Claire The path of true love is seldom straight!

A beat

Jim Did you see her laughing at everything he said?

Claire Well, you do, early on, don't you?
Jim Pathetic jokes and all!
Claire Well, she's infatuated by him, isn't she?

A beat

Jim Are we in the right place?
Claire Why?
Jim Quiet.
Claire Well, we could have sat out there and looked around the shops, but I thought you wanted to see the planes. We should be boarding soon anyway.

Jim stands and looks at the fourth wall

Jim Looks a bit grim out there.
Claire I've enjoyed it.
Jim Looks like there's some weather heading over here.
Claire Saw some stuff, didn't we?
Jim Black as hell out here!
Claire You got some stuff on the Kennedy killing, didn't you?
Jim I just got a...
Claire I thought you weren't interested in any of that?
Jim It's just something to read...
Claire If you ever have time.

Bing-bong! Over the tannoy we hear that the BA flight is delayed

Jim Hang on...
Claire Is that boarding?
Jim Ssssh!
Claire What's it say?
Jim Hang on!
Claire Ssssh!
Jim Missed it! That's with you!

Music

Fade Lights

Scene 8

Dallas Fort Worth. Two hours later, evening

Jim has had a drink. Claire is standing looking out into the fourth wall

Claire It's very black out here.
Jim Yes?
Claire Very black.
Jim Mmm!
Claire Bad weather coming in. I bet that's why we're delayed.
Jim Mmm!
Claire I don't think I've ever seen the sky so black.

A beat

Jim I'm … er … thinking of leaving.
Claire What?
Jim I'm thinking about leaving.
Claire Oh!
Jim Yes.
Claire Good timing.

A beat

Jim Yeh yeh, I'm thinking about moving out.
Claire Where to?
Jim Get a flat.
Claire A flat?
Jim Yes.
Claire And live on your own?
Jim Yes.
Claire A bachelor pad, is it?
Jim No, it's just a flat.
Claire Oh, right!

A beat

Jim I've been thinking about it for a long time.
Claire Well, I knew there was something, but…

A beat

Jim It's been coming…

Claire Has it?
Jim Yes!
Claire Has it really?

Jim is frustrated by the conversation

Jim This is why…
Claire Is it?
Jim I can't talk to you any more.

A beat

Claire You're not easy to live with.
Jim Neither are you!
Claire Oh, right!
Jim I never said I would be!

A beat

Claire And what are you going to do with your love nest? Take lots of young women back? And then what, fuck them senseless?
Jim Jeeez…
Claire That'll be good.
Jim Yes, it will!
Claire Be a first for you!

A beat

Jim Well, it depends who you're with, doesn't it?
Claire Well, you get breathless cutting the lawn, so…

A beat

Jim I'll buy an exercise bike.
Claire Sounds like you're going to need one!

A beat

Jim I'm serious, Claire!

A beat

Claire Will you be having a black leather sofa in the flat because you can take

that one out of the study! Do you think you'll be able to shag on that? Or will it be bad for your back? You've never been able to sleep on leather, have you, it makes you sweat, doesn't it?
Jim I'm serious!
Claire I've got the message.
Jim I am.
Claire I've heard you.
Jim Good.
Claire It's been coming.
Jim It has.
Claire Like you said…
Jim I can't go on like this…

A beat

Claire So she'll move in with you then, will she?
Jim Who?
Claire This Zoë!
Jim Oh, please…!
Claire Come on…?
Jim Please!
Claire Come on…?
Jim Listen!
Claire Isn't she the reason?
Jim Please!
Claire You're kidding yourself.
Jim This isn't about Zoë…
Claire Isn't it?
Jim No…

A beat

Claire Twenty-one is she, twenty-three?
Jim It's got nothing to do with her!
Claire You keep saying…
Jim It's about me and you!
Claire Is it?
Jim It's about how we put up with each other!
Claire And that's what we've been doing, is it?
Jim You know we have!
Claire That's right.
Jim Boring each other to death!

A beat

Claire How long will it be before you're bored by her, then?
Jim It's got nothing to do with her.
Claire How long will it be?
Jim It's nothing to do with her.
Claire How long will it be before she's bored by you?
Jim It's nothing to do with Zoë!
Claire How long will it be, do you think?
Jim It's got nothing to do with her!

A beat

Claire I'll give her a month.

Music

Fade Lights

Scene 9

Dallas Fort Worth. One hour later, night

Lights come up on Claire, who is now seated and feeling the tension and Jim who is standing at the side of the stage

Jim This is crazy!
Claire That's right.
Jim Bloody madness this, look at the weather!
Claire Is that all you're interested in?

A beat

Jim We've been going wrong for months, years! You never have any time for me, you don't stimulate me, you're not sexy with me!
Claire Anything else?
Jim Oh, shut up!

A beat

Claire So you've had sex with her, then?
Jim Listen ... it's got nothing to do with Zoë!
Claire So you have had sex with her?
Jim No, I haven't!

Claire You want to?

A beat

Jim This is pathetic!
Claire But you want to?
Jim It's got nothing to do with that…
Claire Liar…
Jim Well, you think…
Claire Liar…
Jim Well, anyway…
Claire Liar!

A beat

Jim I could have had sex with her but I didn't?
Claire Why?
Jim Because…
Claire Because you're married, ha, come on?
Jim Because…
Claire What?

A beat

Jim I don't know why I didn't, to be honest!
Claire Because you haven't got the guts!
Jim Because I'm one of the good guys.
Claire Oh, please!

A beat

Jim Why, would it be better if I had?
Claire I don't care!
Jim Right!
Claire I don't care at the moment.

A beat

Jim I wish you'd've told me that nine months ago.

A beat

Claire But you are going to do, aren't you?

Jim What is this?
Claire In your bachelor pad?
Jim On my black leather sofa!
Claire And portable telly!
Jim Yes, it'll be filthy, and there won't be loads of toilet rolls in the bog, so if you do run out of paper, you'll have to use the shower curtain!

A beat

Claire Nothing new there, I bet you do that anyway!

Music

Fade Lights

Scene 10

Dallas Fort Worth. Five hours later, night

The tiredness and strain is beginning to tell on both of them. Jim is now seated. Claire is looking out towards the audience, she is on the verge of a huge breakdown during the scene

Claire Who is she?
Jim Eh?
Claire Who is she, anyway?
Jim Listen…
Claire Who is she, you don't even know who she is!
Jim Leave it.
Claire Leave it?
Jim Just…
Claire That's rich, that is!
Jim This has been coming…
Claire She flies into our life and suddenly I'm shit…
Jim Nobody said you're shit! It's my problem, it's me!
Claire I'm humiliated at parties, I'm not allowed to come into the office!
Jim Leave it!
Claire You don't talk to me about work.
Jim As if you're interested!
Claire You don't talk to me, full stop!
Jim Why don't you leave it?

A beat

Claire I mean, I hate flying as much as you, but I'm there for you, I always have been, but you've never been there for me! Never!
Jim I have.
Claire You have never been there for me!
Jim I have.
Claire Never when I needed you.
Jim I have.
Claire Always taken me for granted…
Jim I have been there for you.
Claire Twenty-two years…
Jim Here we go…
Claire Twenty-two years…
Jim Here we go!
Claire God Almighty, when I think…
Jim Here we go!
Claire You've pushed me and pushed me…
Jim Well, I won't be pushing you any more.
Claire I could be bleeding to death…
Jim Oh leave it, love!
Claire And you'd never notice.
Jim Oh, melodramatic!
Claire All you do is push me! I've just put up with it.
Jim Like I have to put up with you.
Claire You're on at me all the time, knocking me back, putting me down, Zoë this, we did that… Pushing me…
Jim Oh, dear!
Claire Wanting me to go…
Jim Well, I'm going now, so it's all right, isn't it?
Claire Pushing me!
Jim (*shouting*) I haven't pushed you!
Claire Jesus Christ!
Jim I haven't pushed you, God, woman, I hardly talk to you when we're at home, what have I pushed you to do?
Claire You've pushed me to do things.
Jim Eh?
Claire You've pushed me!

A beat

Jim What things?
Claire Oh!

A beat

Jim What things?
Claire You push and push!
Jim What things?

Claire is completely broken

Claire Oh!
Jim You'd better tell me what you've been doing!
Claire Why are you bothered?
Jim What's been going on?
Claire Why are you like this with me?
Jim What things?
Claire Everybody thinks you're such a nice bloke but you're not, you're so cruel...
Jim Claire?
Claire You're cruel!
Jim Claire!
Claire You're killing me...
Jim Tell me.
Claire (*utterly distraught*) I just needed...
Jim What?
Claire Cruel...
Jim You needed what? For God's sake pull yourself together!

A beat

Claire ...somebody...

Silence

Jim What?
Claire I just needed somebody!
Jim Wha...?

A beat

Claire You're cruel with me...
Jim Eh?
Claire I knew you didn't want me...

A beat

Jim Eh...?

Claire Can't you see!
Jim Eh?

A beat

Claire Can't you see what you've been doing?
Jim Jeee.
Claire I don't know where you are from one week to the next…
Jim Jeeee…
Claire You're cruel…
Jim Jeeez!
Claire You've been so cruel with me…
Jim I haven't done anything.
Claire You don't even know when you're doing it! All this stuff about her, every day; phoning you, faxing you, sending e-mails, you having coffees, I know, I know all about it. Your little meetings, Anabelle saw you with her…
Jim I haven't done anything with her.
Claire And what about me … you don't care…
Jim Hey…
Claire You really don't care. I'm forty-three, my little girl's gone and you don't care… (*she is in tears*) you're so, so cruel to me … always have been!
Jim Hey… Claire, I haven't…

A beat

Claire I just needed somebody…

A beat

Jim Who…?
Claire Don't…
Jim I mean when? Jeeee, this is just…!
Claire Oh…!
Jim Who?

A beat

Claire What a bloody…
Jim It's not Steve, is it?
Claire Don't…
Jim It's Steve, isn't it?
Claire Kill me, because I can't live with it?

Jim Is it Steve?
Claire It's not Steve.

A beat

Jim It's not Anabelle, is it?
Claire It doesn't matter who it is, does it?

A beat

Jim It fucking matters to me!
Claire Oh, leave it.
Jim It matters to me!

Music

Fade Lights

Scene 11

Dallas Fort Worth. Five hours later, night

Claire is slightly more composed than previously. Though the emotional outburst has taken its toll on her. Jim looks out into the night. He too looks dreadfully tired

Jim Thirteen hours!

A beat

Thirteen hours now! Every other plane is cancelled, except ours! Our plane isn't cancelled, our plane is delayed according to the screen. There's a hurricane, electrical storms, trees being ripped up and thrown half way across Texas, but our flight isn't cancelled! Our flight is only delayed! Which means that sooner or later the silly bloody pilot is going to decide to fly it! Can you believe it?

A beat

Claire Can we talk…?
Jim That just about sums it up for me!

Bing-bong. An American-accented girl announces embarkation

Claire I think we can check in!

A beat

Jim Oh dear…!
Claire Jim?
Jim Oh, hell…
Claire Jim?
Jim What a bloody…

Jim and Claire make their way slowly off stage

Music

Fade Lights

Scene 12

Manchester. Three days later, day

Zoë is sitting, reading a magazine. She has all her baggage and a small briefcase

Steve enters with two paper cups. He is carrying his computer bag and an overnight bag

Steve Here we are, sorry about the wait, there's only one girl on and a queue a mile long!
Zoë I thought you'd died.
Steve Everybody was pushing in, and when I got there she'd run out of cups.
Zoë Any excuse!
Steve Well, actually, my old limbs wouldn't get me there any faster, so…
Zoë That's more like it…
Steve Hey…?
Zoë Didn't get a sugar, did you?
Steve You did ask, didn't you?
Zoë Well, I did but…
Steve I'll go and get one…
Zoë No, I'll go…
Steve No, no problem. I'll just pop… I knew you'd said something but I was thrown because of the potential international incident. Two ideas in my head at one time, is a case of severe over-crowding at the moment.

Jim enters, he is flustered

Steve is about to depart

Jim Morning!
Steve Thought we were going without you.
Jim No, there's no show without Punch.
Steve I'm going for some sugar, do you want a coffee?
Jim No, I'm on the brandies.
Steve I heard about that hurricane! Oh oh!
Jim If you can fly through that, you can fly through anything!
Steve Nervous?
Jim Shat my pants, but…
Steve Right, sugar… I'll see what I can do.

Steve exits

Jim sits

Jim All right?
Zoë Yeh.
Jim Good!
Zoë Yeh.
Jim It's been a long ten days.
Zoë Yeh!
Jim Well, here we are, then!

A beat

Zoë I was going to text you, but…
Jim I did try to call you, actually, but the phone was off…
Zoë Oh, right!
Jim I mean, it doesn't matter, it's no big deal, I just wanted to hear your voice.
Zoë Oh, well…
Jim Don't worry about it, it's no big deal.
Zoë No, right!
Jim I've got a little bit of something for you.
Zoë Oh, you needn't have…
Jim Oh, yes!
Zoë Everything's big, isn't it?
Jim Especially the hotel bill when I'm not paying but … here we are. (*He feels deep inside his briefcase and pulls out a biography of the Kennedys*)
Zoë Oh, wow!

Jim Just a little something.
Zoë Oh!
Jim Any good?
Zoë Wonderful, thanks very much!
Jim I was going to buy you a Stetson but I thought you'd probably wear it.
Zoë Oh, that's really nice, thank you!

A beat

Jim I hear Brussels was a success.
Zoë I think so.

A beat

Jim Are you OK?
Zoë Yes!

Steve returns with some sugar

Steve The last one...
Zoë Look at this! (*She holds up the present*)
Steve Don't I get one?
Jim This is yours. (*He hands Steve a key ring in the shape of Texas*)
Steve Nice!
Jim It's the thought that counts.
Zoë Actually, will you watch my bag, I'll just have to make a call.
Steve Twenty minutes delayed if you're checking.

Zoë exits

Steve and Jim recline and stretch

All right, then?
Jim Not bad.
Steve How's Annie?
Jim Great...
Steve How's the boyfriend?
Jim Older than me!
Steve A lot in common, then?
Jim Oh, don't!

A beat

Steve Had a good time, then?

Jim Ay, not bad.
Steve Good.

A beat

Jim Is everything all right?
Steve Yes.
Jim I thought I could just detect…
Steve What?
Jim I don't know, I just thought…
Steve No, man, everything's fine! (*He is looking at Steve*)
Jim Is it?
Steve Course it is!

A beat

Jim (*starting to cry*) That's all right, then?
Steve Hey, man?
Jim Sorry, mate.
Steve Hey…
Jim Oh dear…
Steve You OK?
Jim Jet lag, man!
Steve Oh hell!

A beat

Jim Just seeing her again…
Steve Oh man!
Jim Oh hell…
Steve Hey, come on…
Jim This is serious…
Steve I can see that…

A beat

Jim I'm leaving Claire…
Steve What?
Jim I'm leaving her…
Steve Oh, man…
Jim I've told her, I'm moving out!
Steve Oh, man!
Jim Getting a flat!

Steve Oh!
Jim Jeeez...

A beat

Steve Man, are you sure?
Jim Oh ay... We erm... I don't know, I can't go on with her!
Steve Oh dear.
Jim And now I've met Zoë I know it's right!
Steve Oh, right.
Jim I thought it might go away but...
Steve Right, then!
Jim I never felt like this about Claire. Even when I first met her.
Steve Man, you've got twenty odd years...
Jim I know.
Steve That's a religion.
Jim I love her.
Steve Yes.
Jim It's as simple as that...
Steve Man, do you know her?
Jim It's real, mate! Just looking at her and I'm all over the shop...

A beat

Steve Man...
Jim I am...
Steve Oh!
Jim It's the only way I can explain it!

A beat

Steve Man, I think there's been a...

A beat

Jim Wha...
Steve Man...
Jim What?
Steve Oh hell...

A beat

Jim Oh, man!

Steve Sorry.
Jim Eh?
Steve I'm not a King…!
Jim Oh…!
Steve Like you said, dangerous!
Jim Oh…!
Steve I didn't think it was so…
Jim I told you…
Steve I know, but…
Jim I told you as a mate…
Steve I know you did, but…
Jim Fuckin' hell, Steve!
Steve I know, I know!
Jim What did you think I was telling you for, a laugh?
Steve Well, I thought that I was doing you a favour.
Jim Oh, that's the best thing I've ever heard!
Steve Look, listen, I partly did it for you.
Jim Oh, thanks!
Steve I did it for Claire.
Jim That's right!
Steve I did it for the company.
Jim You did it for your fucking self.
Steve It just happened!
Jim I even asked you not to…
Steve You're torturing yourself…
Jim Oh man!
Steve Anyway, you had your chance!
Jim It's not about that, it's about friendship.
Steve Oh!
Jim It is.
Steve Oh!
Jim It is!
Steve So what's changed?
Jim Oh dear…
Steve She's still your mate.
Jim I'm pathetic…
Steve Mate, you can say it's none of my business but don't throw away all you've got…
Jim It's too late for that, Stevie boy…
Steve Listen, if there's ever a trouser factor you can't be a mate with 'em.
Jim So you can only be a mate with ugly women?
Steve Well, I can!

A beat

Jim This is why you wanted her to work for us!
Steve Oh, come on…
Jim Give up, I know you… That's why you tried it on in Spain, and it means nothing to you.
Steve Well, I wouldn't go that far.
Jim I would.

A beat

Steve You don't want to leave Claire … you're made for each other…
Jim So what happened, then, did she just come out with it?
Steve No, we stayed in Manchester because of the weather.
Jim Oh, right.
Steve She … erm … knew this Czech woman or sommat.
Jim Oh, right.
Steve Went to her flat. The three of us. I'm not a King, man.
Jim Oh Jesus!
Steve I'm not a King.
Jim Got a bit further than the kissing this time, then?
Steve Who with?
Jim Bloody hell! (*He begins to cry. He cries hard and then the crying turns into a cackle of laughter. He moves downstage*) Oh, hell, eh? Flying, wonderful, why do I put myself through this!
Steve I only had one night, man…
Jim That's right.
Steve One night…
Jim Yes!
Steve You've had twenty odd years.
Jim That's right.
Steve Not worth it.
Jim That's right.
Steve You're lucky, mate.
Jim I am, aren't I?
Steve You're a King!
Jim King Jim of Shipley!

Steve stands

Steve I'm going to get a drink, do you want one?
Jim No, thanks…

Zoë enters as Steve departs

She senses something is wrong

Zoë Nearly ready.
Jim Yes?

A beat

Zoë You OK?
Jim Me, bloody great.
Zoë Oh, right.

A beat

Jim People, Zoë!
Zoë Yes?
Jim If you want to get the best out of them you have to get to know them. And then what…?
Zoë What?
Jim They let you down.
Zoë Well, I won't let you down.
Jim You silly cow…
Zoë What?

A beat

Jim Steve said you had a good night in Manchester, then?
Zoë Well…?
Jim Said it was a good night!
Zoë Well…

A beat

Jim Well, I suppose we've had a laugh, haven't we?
Zoë We have!
Jim We've had a laugh!
Zoë We can still be mates, can't we?
Jim Can we?
Zoë I hope so.
Jim I hope so and all.
Zoë Good.
Jim Come here, give us a hug!

Zoë slowly walks to Jim and hugs him. Jim then pulls her head back and kisses her

Zoë I do really like you!

Jim But not enough, though, eh, kid?
Zoë I think you're a really funny bloke.
Jim Really funny?
Zoë Yes!
Jim I haven't started being funny yet.
Zoë I do appreciate all you've done for me, you know.
Jim Well, I feel better now.
Zoë That's good, then.
Jim At least I've got kissing far!
Zoë Yes!

A beat

Jim Go and get me a magazine, will you…
Zoë Well, we're nearly boarding…
Jim Go and get me a magazine…
Zoë There's not long.
Jim As a mate!
Zoë Well, it's…
Jim Go and get me a magazine, mate!

A beat

Zoë Right!

A beat

Jim And send Claire some flowers from Inter-Flora. You can do that before we get on, can't you?
Zoë Well, it's…
Jim And put a note in … just write, "love you!"
Zoë Well…
Jim Just do the fuckin' job, mate!
Zoë I will.
Jim And have you got your ticket?
Zoë Yes!
Jim Rip it up! I don't want you to come. Rip it up and go back to the office! I think Darryl in graphics wants some help moving some visuals, you can help him with that. Go on, I'll call you later, if I need anything. And Zoë?
Zoë What?
Jim Can you show me all your receipts from Prague, I just want to check 'em, mate!

Zoë exits sullenly

Steve enters. He is on the mobile phone and is speaking loudly

Steve No, hang on, hang on, Sue, I can't hear you!
Jim Bloody hell!
Steve Go on, what?
Jim Why don't you just shout to her?
Steve (*into the phone*) I thought it was all over?
Jim It is now!
Steve You've booked a what? ... When's this? ... Well, yes, it sounds nice but... Well, let me think about it. Sue, you're breaking up, love... I'll call you later... You're breaking up... I'm losing you! (*He comes off the phone*)
Jim She's always breaking up, isn't she?
Steve Sue's booked us a weekend in Palma!
Jim Oh, nice!
Steve Bloody hell!
Jim Will you be taking Zoë?
Steve Hey, man!
Jim That'd be cosy, wouldn't it?

A beat

Steve She wants you to write her a reference, did she tell you? She's got this job thing, and they're taking her references up. I said she'd probably be better off speaking to you about it. You'll write her a good reference, won't you?

A beat

Jim Can you live with her going, though, Steve?
Steve She's dead as far as I'm concerned.
Jim Or will it break your heart?
Steve Can you live with her staying?
Jim She's dead as far as I'm concerned and all! She can go and rot, so it doesn't matter to me either way!

A beat

Steve Where is she?
Jim She's doing me a little job.
Steve Right!
Jim I've sent her back to the office. She can help Darryl sort some stuff out in the warehouse.
Steve It's needed doing for ages that warehouse. It's a mess in there.

Jim It is, isn't it.

A beat

Steve Listen, mate.
Jim Forget it.
Steve Hey, man!
Jim I'm serious.
Steve Yeh?

Bing-bong of indecipherable announcement

What's it say?
Jim Sssh!
Steve Hang on…
Jim Sssh!

A beat

Steve What did she say? Is that us?
Jim No idea, mate!

Steve and Jim move across the stage slowly towards the exit

Steve I think that's us.
Jim No idea.

Jim and Steve exit

Music

Fade Lights

Scene 13

Manchester. One week later, night

Claire enters, pushing a trolley with a suitcase on to the stage. She sits by herself and looks at her ticket, she searches through a magazine

As she contemplates, Annie enters, and looks out at the night

Annie You OK?

Claire Yes!
Annie Sure?
Claire Yes!

A beat

Annie Delayed, then.
Claire Yes!
Annie I think the fog's coming in.
Claire Yes!

A beat

Annie Mum?
Claire I'm all right.

A beat

Annie I'm quite looking forward to it.
Claire Where's the villa?
Annie I've got all the details somewhere.

A beat

I don't know how you stood twenty-three years with the same person?
Claire It just seemed simpler.
Annie (*laughing*) Hey, me and you in Cyprus … sun, sea and sex…!
Claire Oh dear!

Jim enters from upstage. He has a flight bag and his computer bag with him, he looks like a man who lives alone

Jim I thought it was you.
Claire Did you?
Jim Finally going to Cyprus, then.
Claire How do you know?
Jim Didn't Annie tell you?
Annie Well…
Jim I've paid for it.

A beat

Claire What do you want, a medal?

Jim Well, no...
Claire So why did you?
Jim I thought it was what you deserved!
Claire Oh, please...
Jim Well, there you go...
Annie Mum!
Jim I didn't actually do anything...
Annie Not here...
Jim Claire, I didn't actually...
Annie Dad?
Claire Well, don't blame me, I didn't stop you.
Annie Mum?
Jim Claire...
Claire It wouldn't have mattered if you had...
Jim I was only...
Claire It was the way you were with me.
Jim I just ... well...
Claire What, fell in love with her?
Annie (*exasperated*) Oh hell!
Claire Did you tell her that?
Jim Come on...
Claire Did you tell her?
Jim Well, actually...
Claire Did you ever tell her how you felt about her?
Jim No... No, I didn't as it happens!

A beat

Claire Oh... Jimbo!
Jim I never told her anything.
Claire Well that was a bit of a mistake, wasn't it?
Jim Well, I couldn't, could I?
Claire Why not?
Jim I'd've felt like a fool.
Claire And you don't feel like a fool for not telling her?
Jim Look, it happens and it hurts, but...
Claire Well, I never thought it would happen to us.
Annie Mum?
Claire Don't you think you'd better tell them next time?
Jim Claire...?
Claire Don't you?
Jim We need to talk about this...

A beat

Claire How's the flat, then?
Jim Hey Claire… Kid!
Claire What you wanted, is it?
Jim Well, I'm sleeping on a camp bed at the moment, so…
Claire The shagging's a bit awkward, then?
Annie Mum, leave it now…
Claire You'll be wanting that sofa, then… You can come and get it when we get back. We're away for two weeks, you know?
Jim I know that, I even booked the bloody villa.
Annie I was going to tell her when we got there, honest.
Jim Whatever!

A beat

Claire Flying alone?
Jim Pisa!
Claire God help the cabin crew!

Bing-bong of an English announcement

Annie That's us!
Jim Dan all right, then?
Annie Yes!
Jim That's good, then.

Claire and Annie slowly make their way towards the gate

Have a good flight!
Claire Foggy out there, you know?
Jim It's not, is it?
Claire Terrible!

Claire goes, leaving her hand luggage

Annie stays on stage

Jim What?
Annie I'll talk to her.

Annie exits

Jim is alone, motionless

Jim Cheers, kid! (*He stands and watches them go*)

The bing-bong of indecipherable announcement is heard

Claire comes back on stage

What's up?
Claire Forgot my bag!

Jim hands Claire her hand luggage, they stand holding the bag together for a moment

Claire pulls the bag away from Jim ever so gently, and departs

Jim watches as she goes down the gate. He looks around the departure lounge. He is alone. He sits in hope as the Lights fade to black

Music

CURTAIN

FURNITURE AND PROPERTY LIST

Further dressing may be added at the director's discretion

ACT I

Scene 1

On stage: Airport setting
Jim's book
Steve's newspaper
Eva's large airport novel

Personal: **Eva:** dark glasses

Scene 2

On stage: Airport setting

Scene 3

On stage: Airport setting

Scene 4

On stage: Airport setting

Off stage: Trolley with cases and ski equipment, boarding cards, magazine (**Claire**)

Personal: **Claire:** wrist-watch

Scene 5

On stage: Airport setting

Off stage: Small backpack, tickets (**Annie**)
Flight bag (**Dan**)

SCENE 6

On stage: AIRPORT SETTING

Off stage: Mobile phone, small flight bag, computer bag (**Jim**)
Mobile phone, overnight bag, briefcase (**Steve**)
Bag, chocolate buns (**Zoë**)
Lit cigarette, drink (**Eva**)
Magazine (**Zoë**)

Personal: **Jim:** small bottle of brandy

SCENE 7

On stage: AIRPORT SETTING

Off stage: Mobile phone, bags (**Claire**)
Trolley (**Jim**)

SCENE 8

On stage: AIRPORT SETTING

Off stage: Mobile phone (**Steve**)
Mobile phone (**Zoë**)
2 hot coffees (**Jim**)
Small bottle of brandy (**Zoë**)
Small cabin bag (**Anita**)

SCENE 9

On stage: AIRPORT SETTING
Steve's newspaper
Jim's mobile phone

SCENE 10

On stage: AIRPORT SETTING
Claire's reading matter
Jim's drink

SCENE 11

On stage: AIRPORT SETTING

Coffee
Zoë's bags
Steve's belongings
Jim's belongings containing tablets
Zoë's mobile phone

Off stage: Newspaper, chocolate bun (**Steve**)

Personal: **Jim:** small bottle of brandy

ACT II

Scene 1

On stage: Airport setting
Coffee table
Plastic coffee cup
Zoë's mobile phone

Off stage: Mobile phone (**Steve**)
Reading matter (**Zoë**)
Briefcase, flight bag, mobile phone (**Jim**)
Briefcase containing magazine (**Jim**)
Magazine (**Zoë**)

Personal: **Eva:** piece of paper with number on it

Scene 2

On stage: Airport setting

Off stage: Overnight bag, briefcase, mobile phone (**Steve**)
Mobile phone (**Jim**)

Scene 3

On stage: Airport setting
Claire's belongings & boarding cards

Scene 4

On stage: Airport setting

SCENE 5

On stage: AIRPORT SETTING

SCENE 6

On stage: AIRPORT SETTING

SCENE 7

On stage: AIRPORT SETTING

On stage: **Claire**'s posh carrier bags
Hand luggage

SCENE 8

On stage: AIRPORT SETTING

SCENE 9

On stage: AIRPORT SETTING

SCENE 10

On stage: AIRPORT SETTING

SCENE 11

On stage: AIRPORT SETTING

SCENE 12

On stage: AIRPORT SETTING
Zoë's magazine, baggage, small briefcase

Off stage: 2 paper cups, computer bag, overnight bag (**Steve**)
Briefcase containing biography of Kennedys (**Jim**)
Sugar (**Steve**)
Key ring (**Jim**)
Mobile phone (**Steve**)

SCENE 13

On stage: AIRPORT SETTING

Off stage: Trolley with suitcase, hand luggage, ticket, magazine (**Claire**)
Flight bag, computer bag (**Jim**)

LIGHTING PLOT

Property fittings required: nil
1 interior. The same throughout

ACT I, SCENE 1

To open: Airport lighting - evening

Cue 1 Music at end of scene (Page 1)
Fade lights

ACT I, SCENE 2

To open: Airport lighting - evening

Cue 2 Music at end of scene (Page 2)
Fade lights

ACT I, SCENE 3

To open: Airport lighting - evening

Cue 3 Music at end of scene (Page 6)
Fade lights

ACT I, SCENE 4

To open: Airport lighting - day

Cue 4 Music at end of scene (Page 10)
Fade lights

ACT I, SCENE 5

To open: Airport lighting - evening

Cue 5 Music at end of scene (Page 12)
Fade lights

ACT I, SCENE 6

To open: Airport lighting - night

Cue 6 Music at end of scene (Page 18)
Fade lights

ACT I, SCENE 7

To open: Airport lighting - day

Cue 7 Music at end of scene (Page 20)
Fade lights

ACT I, SCENE 8

To open: Airport lighting - evening

Cue 8 Music at end of scene (Page 27)
Fade lights

ACT I, SCENE 9

To open: Airport lighting - day

Cue 9 Music at end of scene (Page 31)
Fade lights

ACT I, SCENE 10

To open: Airport lighting - evening

Cue 10 Music at end of scene (Page 35)
Fade lights

ACT I, SCENE 11

To open: Airport lighting - night

Cue 11 Music at end of scene (Page 39)
Fade lights

ACT II, SCENE 1

To open: Airport lighting - evening

Cue 12 Music at end of scene (Page 48)
Fade lights

ACT II, SCENE 2

To open: Airport lighting - day

Cue 13 Music at end of scene (Page 51)
Fade lights

ACT II, SCENE 3

To open: Airport lighting - day

Cue 14 Music at end of scene (Page 54)
Fade lights

ACT II, SCENE 4

To open: Airport lighting - day

Cue 15 Music at end of scene (Page 54)
Fade lights

ACT II, Scene 5

To open: Airport lighting - day

Cue 16 Music at end of scene (Page 55)
Fade lights

ACT II, Scene 6

To open: Airport lighting - evening

Cue 17 Music at end of scene (Page 56)
Fade lights

ACT II, Scene 7

To open: Airport lighting - evening

Cue 18 Music at end of scene (Page 58)
Fade lights

ACT II, Scene 8

To open: Airport lighting - evening

Cue 19 Music at end of scene (Page 62)
Fade lights

ACT II, Scene 9

To open: Airport lighting - night

Cue 20 Music at end of scene (Page 64)
Fade lights

ACT II, Scene 10

To open: Airport lighting - night

Cue 21 Music at end of scene (Page 68)
Fade lights

ACT II, Scene 11

To open: Airport lighting - night

Cue 22 Music at end of scene (Page 69)
Fade lights

ACT II, Scene 12

To open: Airport lighting - day

Cue 23 Music at end of scene (Page 79)
Fade lights

ACT II, Scene 13

To open: Airport lighting - night

Cue 24 **Jim** sits down (Page 83)
Fade lights to black

EFFECTS PLOT

ACT I

Cue 1 To open Scene 1 (Page 1)
Tannoy calling out Spanish departure times

Cue 2 **Jim**: "Bollocks!" (Page 1)
Music

Cue 3 To open Scene 2 (Page 2)
Tannoy delivers Spanish announcements again

Cue 4 **Jim**: "I'm going to get it next time." (Page 2)
Music

Cue 5 **Steve**: "To the bar, then, to see Janice and Sally?" (Page 6)
Tannoy announcements by Spanish voice

Cue 6 **Jim**: "I'm laughing my head off!" (Page 6)
Music

Cue 7 **Jim** and **Claire** laugh (Page 10)
Music

Cue 8 To open Scene 5 (Page 10)
Crash of thunder

Cue 9 **Annie** laughs and watches **Dan** exit (Page 12)
Music

Cue 10 **Steve**: "…might throw him out of sequence." (Page 14)
Tannoy announcement by German voice

Cue 11 **Steve** and **Zoë** turn to exit (Page 14)
Sound of aircraft passing overhead

Cue 12 **Eva** walks away from **Jim** (Page 16)
Sound of aircraft passing overhead

Cue 13 **Zoë** laughs at **Jim** (Page 18)
Music

Cue 14 **Jim** exits (Page 20)
Music

Cue 15 **Zoë**: "Sorry." (Page 23)
Tannoy announcement by French voice

Cue 16 **Anita**: "…enjoy your stay in Brussel, uh?" (Page 27)
Music

Cue 17 **Jim**: "…I'll go through the bloody roof." (Page 31)
Music

Cue 18 **Claire**: "Aye, get me a bloody big brandy!" (Page 35)
Music

Cue 19 **Jim** downs one bottle (Page 38)
Tannoy announcement

Cue 20 **Jim** walks purposefully off (Page 39)
Music

ACT II

Cue 21 To open Scene 1 (Page 40)
Tannoy announcements

Cue 22 **Zoë**: "Well…" (Page 41)
Tannoy flight announcement in German

Cue 23 **Jim** and **Zoë** laugh (Page 48)
Music

Cue 24 **Steve**: "Well, I do as it happens but…" (Page 50)
Tannoy announcement in English

Cue 25 **Steve** and **Jim** exit (Page 51)
Music

Cue 26 **Claire**: "I hope somebody shoots you!" (Page 54)
Music

Cue 27 **Jim**: "Yeee haaaa!" (Page 54)
Music

Cue 28 They laugh (Page 55)
Music

Cue 29 **Claire** hugs **Annie** (Page 56)
Music

Cue 30 **Claire**: "If you ever have time." (Page 58)
Tannoy announcement that BA flight is delayed

Cue 31 **Jim**: "That's with you!" (Page 58)
Music

Cue 32 **Claire**: "I'll give her a month!" (Page 62)
Music

Cue 33 **Claire**: "…I bet you do that anyway!" (Page 64)
Music

Cue 34 **Jim**: "It matters to me!" (Page 68)
Music

Cue 35 **Jim**: "That just about sums it up for me!" (Page 68)
Tannoy announcement by American-accented girl

Cue 36 **Jim** and **Claire** exit (Page 69)
Music

Cue 37 **Steve**: "Yeh?" (Page 79)
Tannoy indecipherable announcement

Cue 38 **Jim** and **Steve** exit (Page 79)
Music

Cue 39 **Claire**: "God help the cabin crew!" (Page 82)
Tannoy English announcement

Cue 40 **Jim** stands (Page 82)
Tannoy indecipherable announcement

Cue 41 Lights fade to black (Page 83)
Music